蓮塘珍藏中國鼻煙壺

THE LOTUS POND

COLLECTION OF CHINESE SNUFF BOTTLES

蓮塘珍藏中國鼻煙壺
THE LOTUS POND
COLLECTION OF CHINESE SNUFF BOTTLES

Clare Chu 編著

圖書在版編目（ＣＩＰ）數據

蓮塘珍藏中國鼻煙壺 ： 漢英對照 ／（美）柯莉爾瞿
(Clare Chu) 編著. -- 北京 ： 文物出版社，2021.10
ISBN 978-7-5010-7228-6
Ⅰ．①蓮… Ⅱ．①柯… Ⅲ．①鼻煙壺－收藏－中國－
漢、英 Ⅳ．①G262.8
中國版本圖書館CIP資料核字（2021）第193444號

編　　著：Clare Chu	Author and Scholar : Clare Chu
策　　劃：蔡榮發	Producer : Jones Tsai
出　　品：ＣＡ藝術書冊 www.cabookpublishing.hk	Presentation : CA Book Publishing www.cabookpublishing.hk
統　　籌：陳麗香	Project Director : Rosanne Chan
中文撰文：蔡榮發	Chinese Author : Jones Tsai
制　　作：CA Design	Production : C A Design
設計總監：湯志光	Design Director : James Tong
文章翻譯：蔚　嵐	Articles Translation : Esther Sun
詩詞翻譯：李寶平	Script Translation : Li Baoping
攝　　影：山古影像工作室	Photography : Sankko Image Studio

蓮塘珍藏中國鼻煙壺

The Lotus Pond
Collection of Chinese Snuff Bottles

責任編輯：張小舟	Chief Editor : Zhang Xiaozhou
責任印刷：張　麗	Printing Manager : Zhang Li
出版發行：文物出版社	Publisher : Cultural Relics Press
社　　址：北京市東城區東直門內北小街2号樓	Address : No. 2 Building, Dongzhimennei Beixiaojie, Beijing
郵　　編：100007	Postal Code : 100007
網　　址：http://www.wenwu.com	Website : http://www.wenwu.com
郵　　箱：web@wenwu.com	Email : web@wenwu.com
經　　銷：新華書店	Retail : Xinhua Bookstore
印　　刷：雅昌文化（集團）有限公司	Printing: Artron Culture (Group) Co., Ltd.
開　　本：889mm x 1194mm 1/16	Sizes : 889mm x 1194mm 1/16
印　　張：17.5	Signature : 17.5
版　　次：2021年10月第一版	Publishing Date : October, 2021 First print
印　　次：2021年10月第一次印刷	Printing Edition : First run in October, 2021
書　　號：ISBN 978-7-5010-7228-6	ISBN : 978-7-5010-7228-6
定　　價：1,280.00 圓	Price : 1,280 RMB

目錄　CONTENTS

序

作為國際中國鼻煙壺學會 (ICSBS) 的會長，我非常高興能為這本展示藏品主人豪華收藏中的一些精品鼻煙壺的圖錄作序。

我想介紹一下 ICSBS 的背景，它的工作，以及它對世界鼻煙壺收藏的影響。該組織成立於1968年，當時名為美國中國鼻煙壺學會。這是第一個為中國鼻煙壺收藏家設立的學會，該學會在其季刊上發表有關鼻煙壺的學術文章。1974年，在倫敦會議期間，董事會決定該學會應具有國際性質，將其更名為國際中國鼻煙壺學會，以反映其全球會員和年度大會的情況。奧德爾 (Edward Choate O'Dell) 擔任其創始會長，直到他於1981年去世，我的丈夫 John G. Ford 於1982年至2005年接任。之後，另一位熱心的收藏家 Vincent Fausone, Jr. 接任會長職務，直到2011年。

本學會的使命一直是通過組織觀看和觸摸世界各地的博物館和私人收藏的鼻煙壺來培養和提高鑒賞水平。經銷商一直是本學會會員的重要組成部分，因為他們不僅向我們的會員提供鼻煙壺，而且通過參加年會和其他會議，成為我們獲取關於鼻煙壺源流遞藏和其他專業知識的主要資訊來源之一。他們的參與使會員能夠看到、觸摸和購買市面上最好的鼻煙壺作品。本學會還為會員提供了與其他收藏家會員建立關係和分享資訊的機會，使他們對自己的收藏在已知的基礎上有了更多的瞭解。這也包括在我們的網站論壇 — www.snuffbottlesociety.org, Facebook, Instagram 和 Twitter 上的討論。

應該特別讚揚柯莉爾瞿 (Clare Chu) 女士，是本圖錄的作者。她以極大的熱情完成了這項艱巨的任務，並從她的職業生活中抽出數不清的時間來進行研究和撰寫說明，而這些說明條目通過她的文字給出了非常具有說服力的信息。這本圖錄所囊括的藏品涉及廣泛的風格和題材，對作者充滿挑戰；而柯莉爾瞿文采斐然的藏品說明則充分展現了她的學術造詣。

我非常感謝藏品主人的慷慨，出版了這本精美的圖錄。

貝絲・福特
國際中國鼻煙壺學會
會長

INTRODUCTION

It is with great pleasure that I, Berthe H. Ford, president of the *International Chinese Snuff Bottle Society (ICSBS)*, write an introduction to this catalogue illustrating some of these beautiful bottles from the Lotus Pond Collection.

I'd like to give a background of the *ICSBS*, its work, and its influence on the world of snuff bottle collecting. The organization was founded in 1968 as the *Chinese Snuff Bottle Society of America*. It was the first society to honor Chinese snuff bottle collectors and the society published scholarly articles about snuff bottles in its quarterly Newsletter. In 1974, during the London Convention, the Board of Directors decided that the society should take on an international character by changing its name to the *International Chinese Snuff Bottle Society*, reflecting both its worldwide membership and the annual conventions. Edward Choate O'Dell served as its founder-president until his demise in 1981 when John G. Ford, my husband, took over from 1982 through 2005. Then, Vincent Fausone, Jr., another dedicated collector, took over the presidency until 2011.

The mission of this society has always been to educate and raise the level of connoisseurship by seeing and handling snuff bottles around the world housed in museums and private collections. Dealer members have always been an important part of the membership as they not only provide bottles to our membership but are a major source of information related to provenance and expertise while attending conventions and meetings. Their participation enables members to see, handle and buy the best available bottles. The society also gives members the opportunity to establish relationships and share information with other collector-members to increase knowledge of their own collection above what one may have already experienced. This also includes discussions on our website forum, www.snuffbottlesociety.org, Facebook, Instagram, and Twitter.

Special accolades should be given to Clare Chu for accepting our request to be the author of this catalogue. She met the exacting task with great enthusiasm and spent untold hours out of her professional life to research and write entries that are tellingly revealed in her words. The catalogue entries are a testament to her scholarship, which is always challenging when writing about a wide range of styles and subject matter as observed in this elegant book.

I thank the owner of the collection profusely for his generosity to publish this brilliant catalogue.

BERTHE H. FORD
President
The International Chinese Snuff Bottle Society

前言

二十世紀九十年代初，我在香港的一個拍賣會上第一次見到本書藏品的主人。藏家的情趣反映在他們的藏品中，他也不例外。他的鼻煙壺收藏展現了個人對一流工藝美術品所作出的回應。選擇藏品的標準不是材料，而是它們共同的美感和品質，以及他所識別的對他而言非常重要的一些核心特徵。相應地，本書也沒有按照鼻煙壺的材質，而是依據它們的地點、流派或製作工坊進行編排。如果讀者需要按照材質來查閱本書中的鼻煙壺，則可參考書末的縮略圖索引。

當藏品主人和他的妻子歡迎我來到他們家，開始挑選鼻煙壺時，我立即意識到了這個收藏的高品質；但每個作品獨特的美，以及最終整個系列的美，則是在我打開一個又一個的盒子時逐漸展現的。因此，我選擇鼻煙壺時採用的標準是主觀的，而讀者們可以自行決定他們在多大程度上同意我的這些標準。

對收藏家而言，吸引人的不僅是這些鼻煙壺的品質和美感，還有整個收藏所凸顯的藏品主人的淵博學識。這反映了他對其藏品的文化意涵的關注。例如，所選藏品中有大量的御製鼻煙壺，還有一組有銘詩的鼻煙壺作品，而藏品主人則花費時間和金錢請人將題銘的內容譯成英文。在這本圖錄中，我們還在適當之處加上了一些吊墜，作為對某些鼻煙壺作品的補充，這也是藏品主人的想法。我非常感激他這種對細節的關注，這讓我們都能更加全面地欣賞他的收藏。

我非常感謝藏品主人允許我自由地選擇藏品，儘管我也承認他對特定鼻煙壺的熱情為我的選擇提供了一些溫和的、方向性的暗示。很巧的是，我們曾一起欣賞讚歎一件瑪瑙巧雕鼻煙壺，甚至還討論了石頭中抽象的自然紋理給我們帶來的不同感受；而這件作品的照片一經放大，就成了本書的封面。這就是志同道合的收藏家分享他們的收藏時所擁有的樂趣。我和藏品主人對鼻煙壺上描繪的自然景物以及立體雕塑的形式都有著旗鼓相當的熱情和親切感，這也使得我在決定將哪些作品包括在內，以及將哪些作品勉強放回它們的盒子裡時做出了一些艱難的決定。通過這本圖錄，一個豐富而奇妙的世界被展示給其他藏家，供諸位欣賞。當讀者翻開書頁時，他們會看到，過去的東西蘊藏在我們每個人的心中，而像《蓮塘珍藏中國鼻煙壺》這樣的藏品，則讓我們能夠在這個世界中駐留片刻。

CLARE CHU (柯莉爾瞿)
國際中國鼻煙壺協會
主任兼秘書
期刊編輯

PREFACE

I first met the owner of this collection, in the early nineties in Hong Kong, when we were attending an auction. The sensibility of a collector is mirrored through their collection and the owner of the Lotus Pond Collection is no exception to this rule. His collection of snuff bottles is a personal response to works of art at the highest level. It is not determined by material but by a commonality of beauty and quality, and by his recognition of those core characteristics that are important to him. In keeping with this, the bottles in this book are not grouped by material, but by location, school, or workshop. The thumbnail photo index at the end of the book will aid readers to reference bottles by material should they so wish.

When I was welcomed by the owner of the collection and his wife into their home and began the process of selecting bottles, the high level of quality was immediately apparent to me, but the beauty of the individual bottles, and ultimately of the whole collection, was a gradual unfolding as I opened box after box. The criteria for my selection of bottles for this catalogue is therefore subjective and it is up to the reader to decide how far they may share these.

It is not only the quality and beauty of the bottles that will hold appeal for collectors but also the scholarly expertise which is apparent throughout the collection. This reflects the interest that the owner of the collection has in the cultural significance of his collection with, for example, its abundance of bottles from the imperial workshops, and the group of bottles with poetic inscriptions that he has taken the time and expense to have translated. It was also his idea to complement some of the bottles by adding pendants to this book where they are well suited. I greatly appreciate such attention to detail as it allows us all to fully enjoy his collection.

I am extremely grateful to the owner of the collection for allowing me the freedom to make the selection of bottles, although I also acknowledge the gentle nudges in direction that he made in his enthusiasm for specific bottles. It was fortuitous that together we marvelled over the silhouette agate that, once photographically enlarged, became the cover of this book, even as we discussed what the abstract natural inclusions in the stone evoked differently for us. Such is the joy of like-minded collectors sharing their collections. My passion for depictions of the natural world on snuff bottles and my affinity for three-dimensional sculptural forms are equal to his which made for some tough decisions on what bottles to include, and what to reluctantly return to their fitted boxes. Through this book, a world that is rich and wondrous is made accessible to other collectors for their delight. As the reader turns the pages, they will see that the past is embedded in all of us, and collections such as the Lotus Pond Collection allow us to inhabit that world for a moment in time.

CLARE CHU
Director and Secretary
Editor of the *Journal*
The International Chinese Snuff Bottle Society

自序

承蒙國際中國鼻煙壺學會會長貝絲‧福特 (Berthe Ford) 的認可與推薦，終於能順利完成《蓮塘珍藏中國鼻煙壺》圖錄的刊行，實在萬分感謝。

同時，由衷感謝世界著名鼻煙壺專家 Ms. Clare Chu 在圖錄製作過程中，不吝賜教，以其專業的角度，協助本人從藏品中挑選精品，並為每件鼻煙壺撰寫精闢的英文解說，讓讀者能對鼻煙壺有更深入的認識。

個人收藏鼻煙壺的緣起，在於1993年一次公務出差。那次在舊金山中國城一家專營中國及日本古董的老店 Dragon House，初次見識鼻煙壺及玉器，馬上深受吸引，繼而愛不釋手，引發日後對這類古董的興趣與追求。

1994年，在因緣際會下，加入了第一屆中國鼻煙壺學會，結識了不少同好。往後的日子裏，我積極地搜集更多有關鼻煙壺的中外專業書籍與圖錄，藉此增進知識，此中過程，誠樂事也。

1995年，初訪當時仍稱勁松民間工藝品舊貨市場的北京古玩城，巧遇一位年輕卻資歷頗深的古玩專家 David Lu。他的引介與解說，令我對鼻煙壺細緻多樣的材質與分類，有了深入的認識；甚至一些較深奧的學問，如雕工鑑賞及年代判別等，都有機會涉獵，實屬難能可貴，心中欣喜萬分。

當時的中國古玩市場，剛興起一股收藏風氣，各地的大型拍賣公司如瀚海、嘉德、天津文物等活躍營運，儼如雨後春筍，更會不定期舉辦古玩及書畫拍賣會，盛況一時。

因此我在工作之餘，養成了流連拍賣場的習慣，藉此物色心儀的目標。在拍賣會期間的空檔，也會抓緊時間，逛遍北京新落成的古玩城、琉璃廠等地方。

這段期間，我結識了多位古玩專家，其中有琉璃廠的李德正先生。他專精於北京料器及各式鼻煙壺，以及各種具玩賞或收藏價值的古玩，如瑪瑙、玉器、琺瑯等。自從認識他以後，每次當我路過北京，必定會上門拜訪，專程討教。

此後我擴展了我的藏品種類，除鼻煙壺外亦開始收藏明清玉器、文玩掛件、蘇作巧雕、瑪瑙掛件等。經多年來的努力，也累積了數百件之譜，期望完成這次鼻煙壺圖錄後，再製作另一本圖錄，將這幾年來收藏的玉器或瑪瑙件中的精品選出，一併來做個記錄。

1999年，經朋友介紹，我加入了國際中國鼻煙壺學會。當時註冊會員約有六七百人，遍布世界各地。學會每年在世界不同城市舉辦會員交流及學術研討會，也定期發表刊物。入會之後，我參加過英國倫敦、美國洛杉磯、新加坡、中國香港及北京等多次年會，每次都會隨大會參觀各大博物館，如倫敦大英博物館、紐約大都會博物館、舊金山博物館、北京故宮博物院及上海博物館等。眼歷過這許多琳琅滿目的精彩展品，不但擴大了見識，還刺激了追求的意欲。說回年會，無疑是一個結識世界各地同好的良機；另一方面，又可參與同場舉辦的經銷活動，那是由多家國際著名的鼻煙壺經銷商在會場營辦的展示廳，展銷數量龐大而精彩多樣的精品。我從這些觀賞及買賣活動中，獲益匪淺，也奠定了收藏鼻煙壺的興趣與方向。

年會舉辦期間，學會也安排觀賞當地收藏家的藏品，這些藏家中，不乏世界知名人士，例如在新加坡那年，我們便拜訪新加坡大收藏家劉修敬 (Denis Low) 先生，欣賞他的珍品；香港年會期間，有幸一睹鼻煙壺專家莫仕撝 (Hugh Moss) 先生的精美藏品，也屬機會難逢。此後，我便時常關注世界級拍賣公司如蘇富比、佳士德及邦翰斯等舉辦的鼻煙壺專場，每當發現心儀的藏品，若認為值得收藏，便會參與競拍，偶爾遇到強勁的對手，競價抬得太高，那便雖不捨也要放棄。直至今時今日，我對競拍的最後標價，還是會感到難以掌握，不知如何抉擇。

我的收藏途徑及經驗，除了拍賣場競標外，也會從世界各地知名的經銷商處搜羅。眾所周知，每當有重要拍賣會舉行，各地商家便會同期舉辦古董展銷會，如北京古玩城、香港古董展銷會等，提供觀摩及收藏鼻煙壺的好渠道，真是琳琅滿目，美不勝收。

歷年來我收藏了約五百多件鼻煙壺。這幾年來，當我檢視這批藏品，覺得是時候為它們做個收藏記錄了。這部收藏圖錄取名《蓮塘珍藏中國鼻煙壺》(The Lotus Pond Collection of Chinese Snuff Bottles)，因我祖籍為福建蓮塘。經鼻煙壺專家 Ms. Clare Chu 精心挑選、指導與建議，我們將這批鼻煙壺分類為：造辦處官窯、北京作坊、蘇州作坊、楊州作坊、廣州作坊及其他雜項六類。我自己特別鍾情幾件官窯粉彩瓷胎鼻煙壺、雕工精美的玉質鼻煙壺、蘇作巧雕瑪瑙鼻煙壺及色彩繽紛的料胎鼻煙壺，另外，還會提供幾件蘇作巧雕瑪瑙牌片與掛件作參考對比。

收藏藝術品是一個過程，充滿無限驚奇與喜悅。在此非常感謝我太太秀蘭的全力支持，並時刻與我分享當中的樂趣。

還有要感謝統籌陳麗香、設計總監湯志光及其團隊 CA Design 同人，從翻譯、編輯至印刷過程中的全力協助，使圖錄製作能順利完成。

製作過程中遇到的種種困難，均有賴參與工作的全體成員共同努力，才得以克服並圓滿完工，因此我要對大家表達最深的敬意。

蓮塘主人

FOREWORD

My gratitude goes to Mrs. Berthe Ford, president of the International Chinese Snuff Bottle Society. With her kind consent and recommendation, this catalogue of the *Lotus Pond Collection* was made possible and has now been successfully published.

I would also like to thank Ms. Clare Chu, an internationally-renowned snuff bottle expert, who helped me select the items and professionally advised me during the production process. She also very kindly wrote the descriptions for each item in fine detail, providing valuable information about snuff bottles for the readers.

My journey of snuff bottle collecting dates back to 1993 when I went to San Francisco, CA., on a business trip. I had my first encounter with snuff bottles and jade objects in a shop called Dragon House in Chinatown that sold Chinese and Japanese antiques. It was such a magical moment that I became fascinated with them immediately, resulting in a subsequent age-long pursuit of these precious antique objects.

In 1994, when the Chinese Snuff Bottle Society was inaugurated, I joined them as a founder-member. Over the years, I have made many good friends in the society, and we have shared much information between us. At the same time, I started to collect books and catalogues on snuff bottles both in Chinese and other languages. That in itself was also an engaging and educational experience.

In 1995, I visited Jingsong Antique Market in Beijing for the first time. There I met a young yet well-qualified antique expert named David Liu, who explained to me in detail the materials and categories of snuff bottles. He even shared with me the more intricate knowledge of appreciating both the carving and dating of an object. I learned a lot from him. This was invaluable knowledge and more than I expected.

At that time, the antique market in China was booming and there was a growing trend of collecting rare items. Auction houses like Hanhai, China Guardian, and Tianjin Antique Company were active in the market, organizing regular auctions of antiques, Chinese paintings, and calligraphic works.

I developed a habit of patronizing these auction houses in my leisure time to look for collectibles. I would also hang out in the newly-built antique markets and Liulichang Road in Beijing during any free time between auction sessions.

These visits brought me some new acquaintances in this field, among them Mr. Li Dezheng from Liulichang Road, an expert in glass snuff bottles made in Beijing. His expertise also covers other snuff bottles and collectible antiques such as agate, jade, and enamel pieces. Every time I go to Beijing, I always try to visit him for a good chat.

After that, my collection expanded outside the field of snuff bottles. I started to collect jade ware from the Ming and Qing dynasties, scholarly items and pendants including fine carvings from Suzhou, and agate pendants. I have amassed a few hundred pieces over the years. I hope that another catalogue on jade or agate pieces from my collection can be undertaken now that this one on snuff bottles is completed.

In 1999, I joined the ICSBS through a friend's recommendation. The society had almost seven hundred members at that time, living in different countries. Conventions and seminars were organized around the world every year, and journals were published regularly. I participated in the annual conventions held in London, Los Angeles, Singapore, Hong Kong and Beijing. During the conventions, I took part in the organized museum tours. Among those we visited were the British Museum in London, the Metropolitan Museum of Art in New York, the Asian Art Museum of San Francisco, the Palace Museum in Beijing, and the Shanghai Museum. In Beijing, the Palace Museum was a frequent destination for me to admire the rare enamelled snuff bottles in their collection. These beautiful treasures opened my eyes and encouraged further pursuit. I also made many new friends during the conventions.

The ICSBS always arranged visits to local collectors during the conventions, many of them globally renowned. In Singapore, for example, we visited Mr. Denis Low and had a chance to view his rare collection. In Hong Kong, Hugh Moss's collection was not to be missed, of course. Subsequently, I paid a lot more attention to the dedicated auctions organized by auction houses such as Sotheby's, Christie's, and Bonhams. Whenever I saw a favourite bottle, I would participate in the bidding if I considered it worthy of adding to my collection. However, I would simply let it go when the competition became too fierce, although not without reluctance. Even now, I should say understanding the final hammer price in an auction is still a mystery to me.

Aside from auctions, I acquired my snuff bottles and works of art through other channels. As a standard rule, whenever there is a major auction going on, there are always corresponding exhibitions with dealers displaying and trading antiques. Examples include Beijing Antique City and the Hong Kong Antique Fair, which are good places for searching out and buying snuff bottles.

Over the past few years, whenever I look at the five-hundred-plus snuff bottles I own, I have thought the time was right to create an archive for them. And so, we have this catalogue - *The Lotus Pond Collection*. Lotus pond is pronounced "liantang" in Chinese, which is homophonous with my hometown Liantang in Fujian Province. Ms. Clare Chu handpicked the entries for the catalogue, and made the proposal to divide them into six main categories, namely: Palace Workshops/Official Kilns, Beijing workshops, Suzhou workshops, Yangzhou workshops, Guangzhou workshops, and "Others." My favourites include the *famille-rose* porcelain, carved jade, Suzhou fine-carved agate, and polychrome glass bottles.

The journey of collecting snuff bottles continues to be remarkable. It was always full of surprises and delights. At this juncture, I would like to give special thanks to my wife, Hsiu-Lan, who supports me unreservedly and shares all the joy along the way.

Not to be forgotten, of course, is Ms. Rosanne Chan and her team from CA Design. Their relentless efforts in translating, editing, and printing contributed significantly to the publication of this fine catalogue.

Last but not least, thanks to everyone who has participated in the production process. Your hard work has paid off. Please accept my heartfelt appreciation and respect to you all.

The Lotus Pond Collection

宮廷御製
IMPERIAL
WORKSHOPS

宮廷瓷

清朝雍正皇帝鍾愛瓷器，瓷器的彩繪裝飾以及瓷胎的品質在雍正時期達到了前所未有的高峰，然而，清宮舊藏裡並無雍正時期的瓷胎鼻煙壺。也許因為雍正瓷器不僅注重其裝飾紋樣，亦注重其胎體的透光度。而鼻煙壺小巧，內盛鼻煙，無法展現此特徵，因此幾乎沒有瓷胎鼻煙壺的製作。

其後，乾隆時期，情況大致相同，帶乾隆款識的鼻煙壺多為銅胎畫琺瑯或料胎，瓷胎相對較少。現存所知，唯一一件流傳下來帶雍正款識的瓷胎鼻煙壺在私人藏家手裡，帶胭脂紅料款，八方形，主面繪以花卉紋樣，應在唐英的指導下製成，唐英於1728年出任景德鎮御窯廠的督窯官。

乾隆時期的御用瓷胎鼻煙壺，多現藏於兩岸故宮，個別珍品流存於私人藏家手中。幸運的是，鼻煙壺沿用了官窯落款的習慣，我們得以將這些鼻煙壺明確定為乾隆時期。自十八世紀四十年代始，乾隆皇帝開始下旨景德鎮御窯廠燒造鼻煙壺，此等紀錄沿用至嘉道兩朝。

早期乾隆年製的鼻煙壺由唐英監製，帶有強烈的時代特徵。乾隆九年農曆二月初八日清宮內務府造辦處檔案具體記載下旨燒造形制各異的瓷胎鼻煙壺：

「內務府員外郎管理九江關務（奴才）唐英謹奏為奏明事：『竊（奴才）於乾隆捌年拾壹月貳拾壹日接到內大臣海望寄字，欽奉上諭：着唐英照此掛瓶花紋釉水顏色燒造些各欵式各色鼻煙壺，着其中不要大了，亦不要小了。其鼻煙壺蓋不必燒來。欽此。』欽遵

寄字到（奴才）處着令欽遵辦理。（奴才）接字之日，正值泥土凝凍，歲例停工，各匠俱已回家，窰火亦皆停歇。（奴才）伏念鼻煙壺尚屬小件，坯胎可以烘烤製造，亦便於包裹齎送，因差人至各匠家傅集九江關署，（奴才）親自指點恭擬坯胎數種，并畫定顏色花樣，即於新正齋赴廠署，在民戶燒造粗瓷之茅柴窰價行燒製，並令星夜彩畫，令價造得各欵式鼻煙壺肆拾件，着（奴才）家人齎京恭進。惟是時屆停工，價造匆劇，恐釉水欵式未能仰合聖意，故不敢多造，亦未敢擅動燒造錢糧，（奴才）暫行捐製，恭請皇上教導改正以便欽遵，俟開工之後再行動項製造。」

1756年，唐英因病辭官，不久病故，這或許與景德鎮窰口眾多、污染嚴重的環境有關。乾隆時期的鼻煙壺隨著產量增加，形制多樣化，但大部分的作品均保留了唐英的風格，取用明亮的顏色為地，主體開光為飾，四周環繞圖案化的裝飾紋樣。各面主體圖案的題材每每互相呼應，如一面繪花卉，一面書與花卉相關之詩文，其中不乏乾隆御題。有些設計源於銅胎掐絲琺瑯器，如在瓷胎上描金仿掐絲金線。

這些鼻煙壺的款識相近，底施透明釉，上以礬紅彩於足牆內繪方框，框內書「乾隆年製」四字款，款識工整。

口沿與圈足描金，這是乾隆時期御製瓷胎鼻煙壺的顯著特徵。

在故宮的藏品中，鼻煙壺多置於盒中，常見十件或十二件一組，我們以前認為是根據當時訂燒數量所製，但最新公開的檔案顯示，雖然質量上乘，這些盒子僅作運輸之用，將鼻煙壺從景德鎮安全運往紫禁城。

乾隆晚期至嘉慶時期，瓷器以及瓷胎鼻煙壺流行繪飾文學作品中的場景。有趣的是，我們能從眾多的乾隆與嘉慶款彩瓷上找到一模一樣的畫片。

對此，清宮內務府造辦處為我們提供了十分有意思的新資料。嘉慶三年農曆十月初七日，檔案記載：

「十月初七日將九江關送到五彩磁蓮花碗二十二件（內）（乾隆欵十一件、嘉慶欵十一件，做樣碗，一做係五福堂）呈覽，奉旨將碗內挑出八件交造辦處配。其餘十四件歸入大運磁器內。欽此。挑出八件內（乾隆欵四件、嘉慶欵四件）於十月十六日將五彩磁碗一件配得座呈進刻頭等交瀛台訖。」

當時，從乾隆晚期到嘉慶時期，青花加粉彩描金的裝飾手法十分流行。御製花卉紋題詩鼻煙壺在嘉慶時期逐漸減少，到了道光時期，宮廷中流行其他風格的鼻煙壺。這不僅僅是裝飾紋樣的改變，形制也有所改變，有扁壺形、海棠形等。乾隆末年，模製瓷胎鼻煙壺迅速流行，並盛行於嘉慶和道光時期，彩繪風格也逐漸減弱，改以青花釉裡紅裝飾為主。

PORCELAIN

While Yongzheng porcelain wares were a favorite of the emperor, and the quality of these wares during his reign reached a level not previously achieved by the potters, both in terms of enamel decoration and the fine quality of porcelain, there are no porcelain snuff bottles in the imperial collection from this period. One of the reasons for this may have been that during the Yongzheng period, the finest porcelain was judged not only by the quality of the enameling but also by the translucency of the body. The small size of the snuff bottle, and its use as a container for snuff, did not lend itself to that feature, and few porcelain snuff bottles were likely produced.

Even during the following Qianlong dynasty, this remains true, as the majority of imperially marked snuff bottles were produced in enamel on metal, and in glass, with considerably fewer examples being produced in porcelain. The only known surviving porcelain bottle from the Yongzheng period which bears a Yongzheng reign mark in ruby-red enamel is in a private collection. It is of octagonal faceted form with a delicate floral design on the main side. It was likely produced under the direction of Tang Ying, the supervisor of the imperial kiln complex at Jingdezhen after he was posted there in 1728.

Imperial porcelain snuff bottles from the Qianlong period, are more prevalent in the imperial collection with several superb examples also in private collections. Fortunately, the tradition of applying marks to porcelain wares, including snuff bottles, allows for the dating of these bottles to the Qianlong period. The Qianlong Emperor began ordering snuff bottles made at the Imperial porcelain factory at Jingdezhen during the 1740s and such orders continued throughout his reign and that of his two successors.

The early period of Qianlong-dated snuff bottles is identifiable as the bottles were produced under the direction of Tang Ying himself. In 1743, the eighth year of Qianlong, an imperial order is recorded which is specific, to make forty porcelain bottles of various forms. On the 21st day of the 11th month of 1743, the *Archives of the Imperial Household Workshops* state:

'Tang Ying received a letter from Haiwang with an edict saying: Ask Tang Ying to use the design, color, and glaze of this sedan-chair vase as a prototype to fire some snuff bottles of varied shapes and colors. Remember to make them neither too large nor too small. It is not necessary to fire the snuff bottle stoppers...'.

The response to this edict provides a fascinating insight into the production of imperial porcelain snuff bottles. The Archival Records state:

'Tang Ying in a memorial to the Emperor stated his response and follow-up actions. As it was winter, the clay and raw materials were all frozen. According to the annual tradition, the artisans were on winter vacation. All of them went home and hence, the firing activities at the Kilns were stopped. Upon receiving the edict, Tang Ying immediately summoned skillful potters (from Jingdezhen) to his Customs Offices at Jiujiang. Under his supervision, several different types of biscuits were produced together with matching designs, colors, and patterns. These were instantly sent to Jingdezhen during the Chinese New Year and fired in non-official kilns with rushes and coarse firewood. After the firing, overglazed enamels were hastily applied overnight. A total of forty snuff bottles of different designs were fired and sent to the Capital by family servants. Tang Ying further remarked that as the pieces were produced hastily, he, fearing that the quality, glaze, and shape might not be up to the expectation of the Emperor, did not charge the production expenses to governmental money, but he paid them out of his own pocket. He indicated in the memorial that he was waiting for comments from the Emperor so that he could follow them and make a larger production in the coming spring when the potters came back from vacation. He could then charge the sum to the special vote designated by the Emperor from the income of the Jiujiang Customs Office.' Following edicts indicate that the Emperor was indeed satisfied and ordered that fifty snuff bottles be made every year from then on of the same design.

Tang Ying died in 1756 shortly after a formal request to retire due to ill-health, which may have been connected to the polluted atmosphere of Jingdezhen with its many working kilns. Qianlong period bottles were made in a variety of forms which evolved as production increased, but the essential style that Tang Ying had put in place remained with the majority of bottles being produced with central panels surrounded by decorated borders with a solid background color. Often the decoration within the panels on each main side would complement each other in terms of subject matter, for example, one panel might have a floral design while the reverse would have a poem, sometimes penned by the Qianlong Emperor, that related to the flowers. Other designs were inspired by cloisonné enamels with even the gilded wires of that medium imitated in the porcelain equivalents.

The base marks of these bottles are similar, being well written and in the form of four-character seals painted in iron-red enamel on a transparent glazed base and enclosed along the inner edge of the footrim with an iron-red border.

The mouth and footrims are in all cases gilded. Gilding of the foot and mouth of imperial porcelain snuff bottles seems to be a general feature of bottles made in the Qianlong period.

Although it was previously thought that these bottles were made in sets of ten or twenty since they still exist in the Palace Museums in boxes of those numbers of bottles, it is apparent from the translations of the Imperial Archives that these boxes, albeit of high quality, were essentially packaging for the bottles made in Jingdezhen and sent up to the palace.

Later in the Qianlong period, and continuing into the Jiaqing dynasty, scenes taken from popular literature became popular on ceramic wares and snuff bottles. Interestingly, identical enameled scenes occur with both Qianlong and Jiaqing reign marks. With the translation of the *Imperial Archives of the Household Department* came new and fascinating information relating to this. In 1798, 3rd year of the Jiaqing reign, 7th day, 10th month, the records state:

"Twenty-two pieces of five color porcelain bowls with lotus design were sent to the Court from the Jiujiang Customs Office. Among them, eleven pieces had Qianlong marks and the other eleven had Jiaqing marks. The imperial order said:

'Select eight pieces from the lot and send them to the Imperial Household Workshops to make matching stands. The rest of the pieces should be kept together with these lots from the routine annual orders for porcelain. Respect this.'

Subsequently, eight pieces were selected, four of which bore Qianlong marks and the other four had Jiaqing marks."

At this time, during the late Qianlong into the Jiaqing reign, a style became popular which combined *famille-rose* enamels with underglaze blue designs, detailed in gold enamel. The floral designs with accompanying poems on imperial porcelain snuff bottles seem to have fallen out of fashion during the Jiaqing period and by the Daoguang period, other styles were popular at the court. It was not just the change in design that evolved, but also the change in form ranging from a flattened globular shape to a flattened quatrefoil form. At the very end of the Qianlong period, the fashion for molded porcelain bottles rapidly developed, reaching its height in the Jiaqing and Daoguang periods, along with less use of overglaze enamels and the acceptance of underglaze colors, including underglaze blue and red.

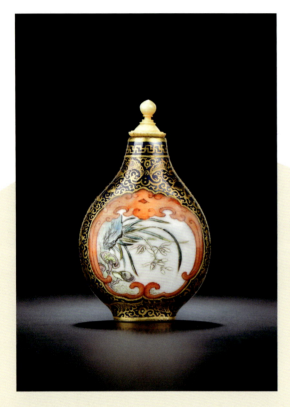
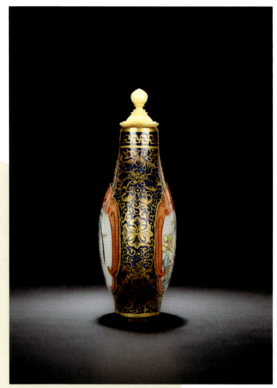

1

清乾隆　藍地描金粉彩開光「富貴長壽」鼻煙壺

鼻煙壺瓷胎，呈扁瓶形。直口，溜肩，腹微鼓，其下漸收，橢圓形圈足。通體施祭藍金彩朵花錦地，腹壁兩面局部留白，留白周緣繪礬紅蝙蝠開光，開光內飾粉彩四季花卉，寓意「富貴長壽」。底部圈足敷飾金彩一圈，圈足內署釉上紅彩「乾隆年製」四字橫書篆體款。

本件鼻煙壺畫工細膩，構圖清妙，顯現出乾隆朝的高度自信。

1736-1756年
高：5 厘米

A porcelain bottle, of flattened, rounded form, with shoulders sloping to a cylindrical neck with a gilded mouth rim, and tapering to a gilded oval foot; decorated using cobalt-blue, *famille-rose* and iron-red enamels with gilding; one main side with a butterfly flitting among leafy, flowering peonies set within a scrolling *lingzhi*-form panel; the reverse with lilies issuing from rockwork beside *lingzhi*; all surrounded by a blue ground, gilded with a design of scrolling lotus flowerheads below a key-fret border at the neck; the base with an iron-red four-character *Qianlong nian zhi* mark in seal script, and of the period.

Imperial, attributed to the Palace Kilns, Jingdezhen.

1736-1756
Height: 5 cm

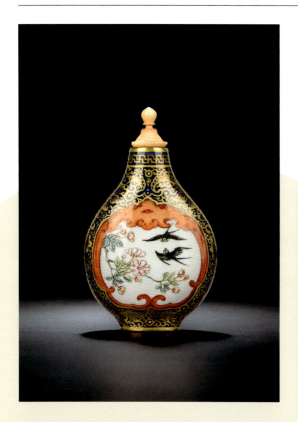

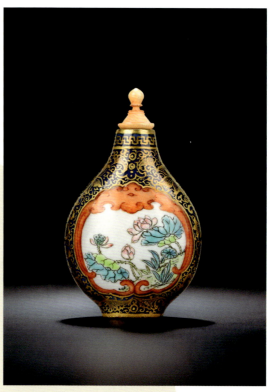

2

清乾隆　藍地描金粉彩開光「河清海晏」鼻煙壺

本件鼻煙壺在造型、構圖、紋樣等方面，俱與前一件風格雷
同。兩者的差異，主要表現在開光內裝飾題材的不同。具體
説，本件鼻煙壺，一面以粉彩勾勒折枝蓮荷，另一面則繪粉彩
雙燕海棠圖。根據「圖必有意，意必吉祥」的圖像寓意，然
則「荷」諧音「河」、「青蓮」取其「清」、「海棠」寄託
「海」、再加上「燕」可同音「晏」，整體綰合起來，便有表
徵四海昇平之「河清海晏」的祥瑞意象了。

1736-1756年
高：5厘米

A porcelain bottle, of flattened, rounded form, with shoulders sloping to a cylindrical neck with a gilded mouth rim, and tapering to a gilded oval foot; decorated using cobalt-blue, *famille-rose* and iron-red enamels with gilding; one main side with a pair of swallows flying above a branch of leafy, blossoming prunus set within a scrolling *lingzhi*-form panel; the reverse with lotus flowers, leaves and pods growing beside a grassy bank; all surrounded by a blue ground, gilded with a design of scrolling lotus flowerheads below a key-fret border at the neck; the base with an iron-red four-character *Qianlong nian zhi* mark in seal script, and of the period.

Imperial, attributed to the Palace Kilns, Jingdezhen.

1736-1756
Height: 5 cm

3

清乾隆　金地粉彩勾蓮紋花瓣形鼻煙壺

本件瓷胎燒結，做花瓣形。直口，頸間交接處飾一匝綠彩連珠
紋，連珠紋上起凸弦紋，下有紅彩浮雕覆蓮紋一圈。豐肩，肩
下急斂，外壁凸起六葉花瓣形開光，通體滿施金彩為地，開光
內壓印皺紋錦地，上飾粉彩浮雕勾蓮紋。橢圓形圈足，圈足內
署釉上紅彩「乾隆年製」兩行四字篆書款。

是件鼻煙壺寓蓮於形，設計巧妙，別出心裁。所施金彩富麗堂
皇，展現濃郁的皇家氣度。

1736-1795年
高：5.1 厘米

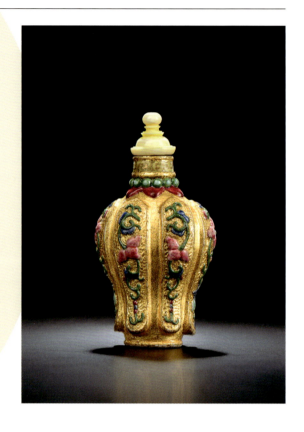

A porcelain bottle, of baluster form, molded and applied with six vertical slightly flaring panels running the length of the body, with rounded shoulders and a cylindrical ridged neck, standing on an oval foot; the stippled body with a gilded ground; each panel molded and decorated in *famille-rose* enamels with a scrolling leafy blossom, the neck with a beaded band between a *lingzhi*-head border and a *leiwen* band; the white-enamel base with a dark-red enameled four-character *Qianlong nian zhi* mark in seal script, and of the period.

Imperial, attributed to the Palace Kilns, Jingdezhen.

1736-1795
Height: 5.1 cm

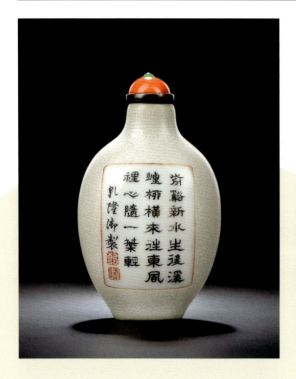

4

清乾隆　白地軋道寶相花御製詩文鼻煙壺

鼻煙壺瓷胎。直口，溜肩，弧腹，腹下漸收，橢圓形臥足。
通體施白地軋道纏枝寶相花錦地，腹壁兩面做矩形開光，開光
內一面以釉上紅彩，書：「前溪新水生，後溪煙柳橫。來往
東風裡，心隨一葉輕。」末鈐：白文「乾」、朱文「隆」
二方印。另一面則繪有四方鈐印，印文內容分別是白文「前
溪新水生」、朱文「後溪煙柳橫」、朱文「來往東風裡」、白文
「心隨一葉輕」等。又臥足周緣飾一圈勾紅金彩，內署紅彩
橫書「乾隆年製」四字篆體款。

考該御製詩，乃乾隆十二年（歲次丁卯，1747年）為其叔父
慎郡王所繪山水小景的題畫詩，即〈題慎郡王山水詩小景十二
幅〉之第三首〈春泛〉。

1736-1756年
高：5.8 厘米

著錄：耿寶昌主編《中國鼻煙壺珍賞》，(香港) 三聯書店，
1992年，133頁。

一面：

「前溪新水生，後溪煙柳橫。來往東風裡，心隨一葉輕。」

末鈐二方印：

白文「乾」、朱文「隆」

另一面四方開光內繪有四方印：

白文「前溪新水生」、「後溪煙柳橫」

朱文「來往東風裡」、白文「心隨一葉輕」

A porcelain bottle, of ovoid form, with shoulders sloping to a cylindrical neck with a gilded mouth rim, and tapering to a gilded oval foot; decorated on one main side within a rectangular panel with a gilded border with a twenty-character inscription in black enamel reading:

"Fresh water springs forth, revives the new stream,
overhanging willow sways freely in the mist,
new water, brisk breeze,
my heart is as light as a leaf."

Followed by 'Imperial composition' and with two red seals *Qian* and *Long*, the reverse with a rectangular panel with four iron-red enameled seals with alternating characters in white and red, each one using a line of the poem; all surrounded by a cream-colored enamel ground engraved with a scrolling floral design of lotus below a key-fret border at the neck; the base with an iron-red four-character *Qianlong nian zhi* mark in seal script, and of the period.

Imperial, attributed to the Palace Kilns, Jingdezhen.

1736-1756
Height: 5.8 cm

Published: Geng Baochang, *The Appreciation of Chinese Snuff Bottles*, Joint Publishing, Hong Kong, 1992, p. 133.

5

清乾隆　粉彩牡丹花卉御製詩文鼻煙壺

瓷胎鼻煙壺。敞口，短束頸，海棠形扁腹，圈足。兩面開光，一面繪粉彩湖石牡丹，另一面書墨彩御製詩〈蒼松牡丹〉的前四句，詩曰：「錦繡堂中開畫屏，牡丹紅間老松青。日烘始識三春麗，歲暮猶看百尺亭。」末繪朱彩鈐印：白文「乾」、朱文「隆」二單字款。開光外飾粉紅地纏枝花卉，近底足處施一圈藍釉連珠紋，圈足金框內署釉上紅彩「乾隆年製」兩行四字篆書款。

是類鼻煙壺畫工俊秀清麗，色彩悅目調和，清宮不乏有配匣成套珍藏的案例。

1750-1795年
高：7.2 厘米

一面書：

「錦繡堂中開畫屏，牡丹紅間老松青。

日烘始識三春麗，歲暮猶看百尺亭。」

末鈐二方印：

白文「乾」、朱文「隆」

A porcelain bottle, of rounded scalloped form, with shoulders sloping to a cylindrical neck with an everted gilded mouth rim, and tapering to a gilded oval foot; decorated using black, *famille-rose* and iron-red enamels with gilding; one main side with a garden of blossoming flowers, the reverse with a twenty-eight character inscription reading:

> "On painted screens in the Hall of Brocade
> is shown fresh red peony with old green pine,
> the bright sun illuminates this clear springtime,
> the pavilion stands aloft throughout the year."

and two red seals *Qian* and *Long*; surrounded by a pink ground with a design of scrolling lotus flowerheads; the base with an iron-red four-character *Qianlong nian zhi* mark in seal script, and of the period.

Imperial, attributed to the Palace Kilns, Jingdezhen.

1750-1795
Height: 7.2 cm

6

清乾隆　粉彩折枝花卉御製詩文鼻煙壺

鼻煙壺扁瓶形。敞口，短束頸，溜肩，肩下漸收，圈足。腹壁兩面做勾紅描金如意形開光，開光內一面飾粉彩折枝花卉，另一面釉上墨書〈虞美人草〉御製詩，詩曰：「一曲虞兮愴別神，徘徊猶憶楚江濱。那知愛玉憐香者，不是當年姓項人。」末繪紅彩鈐印：白文「乾」、朱文「隆」二單字款。開光外施綠地纏枝朵花紋，橢圓形圈足上猶有金彩痕跡，內署釉上紅彩「乾隆年製」四字橫書篆體款。

是件鼻煙壺除造型外，基本與前述作品風格雷同，其紋飾畫工細膩別緻，具典型乾隆朝粉彩韻致。

1750-1795年
高：6.1 厘米

一面書：
「一曲虞兮愴別神，徘徊猶憶楚江濱。
那知愛玉憐香者，不是當年姓項人。」

末鈐二方印：
白文「乾」、朱文「隆」

A porcelain bottle, of rounded form, with shoulders sloping to a cylindrical neck with an everted gilded mouth rim, and tapering to a gilded oval foot; decorated using black, *famille-rose* and iron-red enamels with gilding; one main side with a garden of blossoming flowers; the reverse with a twenty-eight character inscription reading:

> "Such pain in this song for Consort Yu,
> while pacing back and forth I recall the riverbank of Chu,
> who knows the tender heart, only he who cherishes jade and fragrance,
> is this not Mr. Xiang of ages past?"

and two red seals *Qian* and *Long*; each vignette encircled by a gilt border and surrounded by a turquoise ground with a design of scrolling lotus flowerheads; the base with an iron-red four-character *Qianlong nian zhi* mark in seal script, and of the period.

Imperial, attributed to the Palace Kilns, Jingdezhen.

1750-1795
Height: 6.1 cm

7

清乾隆　粉彩仿石釉御製詩文鼻煙壺

鼻煙壺瓷胎，做扁瓶形。撇口，短束頸，溜肩，腹下漸收，平底微凹。通體施仿石釉，腹壁兩面做勾紅描金如意形開光，開光內一面以墨彩繪山水人物圖，另一面則書七言御製詩一首：「架上縹緗玉軸裝，呼童趁夏曝書忙。綠槐庭院無人語，時有天風送古香。」末繪紅彩鈐印：上白文「乾」、下朱文「隆」等二單字款。

乾隆朝瓷器的仿生釉造詣，可謂別開生面。不僅模倣的紋樣惟妙惟肖，而且也流露出高雅清新的藝術氣息。本件鼻煙壺的仿石釉宛如渾然天成，所繪山水人物墨分五色，層次分別，確是一件令人愛不釋手的掌中珍玩。

1750-1795年
高：5.4 厘米

一面書：

「架上縹緗玉軸裝，呼童趁夏曝書忙。
綠槐庭院無人語，時有天風送古香。」

末鈐二方印：

白文「乾」、朱文「隆」

A porcelain bottle, of flattened, rounded form, with shoulders sloping to a cylindrical neck with an everted gilded mouth rim, and tapering to a flat oval foot; decorated using black and brown enamels with gilding; one main side with a scene of a figure standing on a wooden plank bridge over a river, watching a fisherman on the water, the riverbank on one side with trees and large rocks, the other with a pavilion, all set in a mountainous landscape; the reverse with a twenty-eight character inscription reading:

"Scrolls with jade rollers, their yellow silk cases pile high on the shelves,
I summon the boys to seize summertime for basking in books,
not a word is uttered in the courtyard of the green pagoda tree,
the only sound occasional rain from the sky bearing a familiar fragrance."

with two red seals *Qian* and *Long*;
each scalloped vignette encircled by a gilt border and surrounded by a ground with a design of irregular shaped 'pebbles' imitating a quartz conglomerate matrix.

Imperial, attributed to the Palace Kilns, Jingdezhen.

1750-1795
Height: 5.4 cm

8

清乾隆　雕漆嵌瓷開光湖石花卉紋御題詩鼻煙壺

鼻煙壺雕漆嵌瓷，呈扁瓶形。唇口，短束頸，豐肩，肩下漸收，橢圓形圈足。全器以瓷胎為壺膽，外罩雕漆，底足與腹壁兩面鏤空，露出瓷胎，並做上寬下窄的圓弧形開光，開光內一面飾粉彩湖石花卉圖，另一面以釉上墨彩書〈題蔣南沙相國畫屏五景〉御製詩中的〈黃蜀葵〉，詩曰：「色是黃金花是盤，迎風未舞已珊珊。蕊珠宮裡仙人珮，姑射山頭玉女冠。承露更添千葉碧，向陽還有寸心丹。鵝黃淡抹饒深憶，漫作尋常渲染看。」末署「御題」，並繪紅彩鈐印：上「三」（乾）、下「隆」二方朱文款。開光外以剔紅技法，滿飾四方連續團菊錦地紋，兩側開光內並雕有折枝花卉，通體雕工細膩，繁而不亂，展現優美的律動秩序。底署釉上紅彩「乾隆年製」橫書四字篆體款。

1750-1795年
高：6.7 厘米

著錄：耿寶昌主編《中國鼻煙壺珍賞》，（香港）三聯書店，1992年，132頁。

一面書：

「色是黃金花是盤，迎風未舞已珊珊。
蕊珠宮裡仙人珮，姑射山頭玉女冠。
承露更添千葉碧，向陽還有寸心丹。
鵝黃淡抹饒深憶，漫作尋常渲染看。」

末署：
「御題」
並鈐二方印：
朱文「二」（乾）、「隆」

A porcelain and cinnabar lacquer bottle, of flattened ovoid form, with rounded shoulders and a cylindrical neck with everted mouth, tapering at the base to an oval foot; the bottle set with a porcelain panel on each main side, framed within a cinnabar lacquer on wood surround; one side decorated in *famille-rose* enamels with blossoming flowers issuing from rockwork with a bee in flight above, the other with a lengthy inscription in black enamel reading:

"The elegant bloom is colored with gold, shaped like a bowl
as it dances in the breeze, (the flower is like)
the immortals jade pendant kept at the Heavenly Palace,
(the flower is) a crown for the maiden of the celestial
mountain.
Thousands upon thousands of leaves are green with
dewdrops,
always facing the sun is (the flower's) red heart,
it's pale yellow petals strike a chord from an old memory,
like a unique painting is always appreciated."

followed by 'Imperial composition' and two red seals *Qian* and *Long*; the cinnabar lacquer frame carved on the neck and shoulders with a hexagonal diaper pattern, the narrow sides carved with a vertical panel of lotus flowers and leaves, set against a diaper ground, with a floral design within hexagons surrounding the panel on the shoulders and towards the foot; the porcelain base with an iron-red four-character *Qianlong nian zhi* mark in seal script, and of the period.

Imperial.

1750-1795
Height: 6.7 cm

Published: Geng Baochang, *The Appreciation of Chinese Snuff Bottles*, Joint Publishing, Hong Kong, 1992, p. 132.

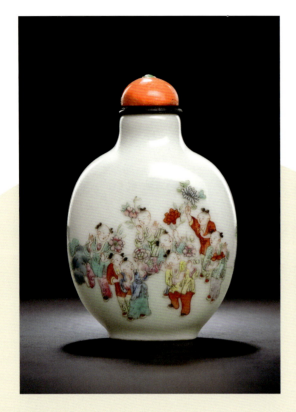

9

清道光　粉彩嬰戲圖鼻煙壺

鼻煙壺瓷胎。直口，溜肩，扁圓腹，腹下漸收，橢圓形圈足。底署「道光年製」紅彩橫書四字篆體款。通體施透明釉，腹壁兩面飾粉彩嬰戲圖。前後嬰戲構圖基本雷同，先以淺綠釉漸層鋪底，兩旁襯以叢草湖石，約略勾勒空間遠近，然後安置童子七、八人，身著短襖寬褲，服色鮮麗多彩，容貌姿態各異，或佇足、或奔跑，每人手持四季折枝朵花，笑容迎面可人，展現一派欣欣向榮的太平景象，亦是道光朝瓷胎粉彩的典型裝飾風格。

1821-1850年
高：6厘米

A porcelain bottle, of bulbous rounded form, a cylindrical neck and with a gilded oval footrim; decorated using *famille-rose* enamels with a continuous scene of boys carrying branches of blossoming flowers for the Spring Flower Festival; the base with an iron-red four-character *Daoguang nian zhi* mark in seal script, and of the period.

Imperial, attributed to the Palace Kilns, Jingdezhen.

1821-1850
Height: 6 cm

銅胎畫琺瑯

十七世紀，身在北京的康熙皇帝收到各國朝貢，其中包括來自歐洲皇室的寶物。法國國王路易十四知道康熙皇帝喜好琺瑯以及西洋珍玩，他挑選了很多琺瑯彩繪製瓷器以及其他琺瑯彩繪珍寶給康熙皇帝。因此，康熙皇帝在紫禁城內設造辦處琺瑯作，開始製作各種銅胎畫琺瑯、料胎畫琺瑯、瓷胎畫琺瑯珍品，其中亦包括鼻煙壺。

1697年，造辦處成立一週年之際，耶穌會法國傳教士白晉從京朝被派前往法國聘請琺瑯工匠回京，但無功而返。在紫禁城內，傳教士郎世寧與馬國賢嘗試繪製琺瑯，但並不成功。有別於雍正‧乾隆兩朝，我們找不到從康熙年間流傳下來的相關檔案記載，但我們普遍認為銅胎畫琺瑯鼻煙壺首創於1716年。再者，同年，廣東總督把一組帶設計的銅胎杯盞送往紫禁城，但據描述，這些杯子並未上彩燒製。這個十八世紀早期的記載十分有趣，但此現象僅見於銅胎畫琺瑯杯。

自康熙年間，琺瑯工匠源源不斷的從廣州被選往北京紫禁城任職。1716年，兩位琺瑯工匠潘淳和楊七章被推荐前往內務府造辦處任職。1719年，法籍琺瑯工匠陳忠信被召向宮中匠人傳授西方琺瑯工藝。可是，雍正年間西洋琺瑯彩的工藝並未達乾隆時期的高峯。

銅胎畫琺瑯鼻煙壺的製作需要在造辦處各個作坊經歷多重工序而成。其銅質壺身成於金屬器作坊，隨後被送至琺瑯作進行繪製與燒製。與其配套的壺蓋和勺子則在其他地方製作而成。

即使沒有文獻記載，從現存銅胎畫琺瑯鼻煙壺的數量可知，其產量比其他種類多。雍正三年，1725年，雍正皇帝下旨造辦處生產兩批鼻煙壺，分別為定例與慶典專用。定例歸皇室日常使用；慶典用器多為春節、端午節等節日所特製。這種訂燒模式在乾隆年間一直沿用。嘉慶年間，據內務府檔案記載，嘉慶皇帝僅下旨製作慶典專用鼻煙壺，並於1813年停止燒製銅胎畫琺瑯鼻煙壺。

根據實物，御製銅胎畫琺瑯鼻煙壺的畫片多具唯一性，很難找到相似的作品。大多數情況下，固定的器形搭配固定的裝飾風格，經典的扁壺便是最常見的例子。球形或圓柱形鼻煙壺多以琺瑯繪飾通景。常見藍料、墨彩、紅料或金彩篆書款。

在北京創燒後不久，銅胎畫琺瑯鼻煙壺很快傳到廣州大量生產。作為一個繁忙的商業港口，廣州不僅僅貿易活動繁榮，在其大街小巷、高樓廣廈中可見密切的文化交流。新貴們踴躍追逐京城貴族精英們所好，其中就包括這各式鼻煙壺。銅胎畫琺瑯鼻煙壺滿足了這些新貴們所追求的身份象徵。與此同時，宮廷作坊生產鼻煙壺供皇帝、宗室和朝臣使用，因此鼻煙壺被視為奢侈品。同時，因為琺瑯工藝由宮內傳教士參與研發，其上常繪飾西洋題材，銅胎畫琺瑯鼻煙壺被視為精美的舶來品。

康熙至嘉慶年間，至少有多達二十位畫工從廣州進入宮廷作坊。他們要參加考核獲取資格，其工作環境惡劣、收入微薄。但假如通過考核，他們便成為高級畫師。這不僅意味著其前程有所保障，其中最優秀的工匠還能獲得皇帝賞賜。據文獻記載，乾隆皇帝下旨命六名廣州琺瑯工匠各製作一件銅胎畫琺瑯鼻煙壺，通過審核者便可入職宮廷作坊。但並無記載是否六人均被錄取。

這種制度使得宮廷作坊與廣州作坊工藝風格互相融合，流出宮廷並最終形成商業主流風格。當時可能在廣州設有皇家銅作坊。儘管我們無法找到確切的文獻記載，十八世紀，乾隆皇帝在全國各地設立玉作坊為其製作玉器珍品，由此可推，他或許在廣州設立了其他門類的皇家作坊。隨著銅胎畫琺瑯在廣州生產，特別生產宮廷器物，廣州本土的琺瑯工匠深深受到了北京琺瑯的影響。因此，乾隆一朝，廣州工匠生產了一系列各式琺瑯器，雖然不及最頂級的京作琺瑯器，仍可媲美當中大部分作品。

ENAMEL ON METAL

During the seventeenth century, the Kangxi Emperor in Beijing received tributes from his counterparts around the world, including from European royalty. The King of France, Louis XIV, sent the emperor numerous enamel on porcelain paintings and other objects when he learned of Kangxi's fascination both for enameling and for Western subjects. Thus, enameling on metals, glass, and ceramics began during his reign when the Emperor set up workshops in the Palace for producing works of art, including snuff bottles.

In 1697, a year after the start of the Palace Workshops, the Jesuit, Bouvet, was sent back to France from the Beijing court to find and recruit enamellers to return with him. Bouvet was unsuccessful, and even the Jesuits Castiglione and Ripa who were established at court, tried their hand at enameling, without much success. Although no archives exist for the Kangxi period (as they do for the following two reigns of Yongzheng and Qianlong), it is understood that the first enamel on copper snuff bottles were produced around 1716. Also, it is known that in the same year the Governor of Guangdong Province sent to the imperial court a group of metal cups on which the patterns were already designed, but which were described as "unpainted and unfired". This can only refer to enamel on copper cups and is an intriguing early eighteenth-century reference.

It became a tradition for enamel artists to be sent from Guangzhou to the court in Beijing during Kangxi's reign and after. In 1716, two enamellers - Pan Chun and Yang Shizhang were sent there to work in the enamel workshops. In 1719, the French enameller Jean-Baptiste Gravereau (also known as Chen Zhongxin) was summoned to pass on Western enameling techniques to the court artisans. However, Western-style enameling during the Yongzheng period did not reach the heights it subsequently did during the Qianlong period.

An enamel on metal snuff bottle would pass through several different workshops in the palace during its manufacture. The copper body would be produced in the metal workshops and then would be sent over to the enamel workshops to be decorated and fired. The stopper and spoon would have been made elsewhere.

Even without any archives, it is evident from the amount of extant enameled metal works of art, that snuff bottles were made in greater numbers than other pieces. The Yongzheng Emperor in 1725, in the third year of his reign, ordered that the workshops produce both "regular" orders and "festival" orders. The "regular" orders were made for imperial use, while the "festival" orders were for festivals such as "New Year" and the "Dragon Boat Festival." This practice continued through the Qianlong period. During the reign of Jiaqing, the *Archives of the Imperial Household Department* show only "festival" orders being made until 1813 when the Jiaqing Emperor ordered an end to the production of enameled bottles for this purpose.

In the majority of cases, most "imperially" made enamel on metal snuff bottles are executed with individual designs, with very few being made more than once. Often the form would dictate the style of decoration, with the classic flattened rounded shape being the usual type. A bulbous or cylindrical form would be more likely to have a continuous scene enameled upon it. The marks are generally executed in seal script and enamel colors of either blue, black, red, or gold.

Enamel on metal bottles were being produced in Guangzhou very quickly after the advent of the industry in Beijing. Guangzhou was a thriving commercial port and it was not only trade goods but culture, which was peddled on its streets and in its mansions. The newly rich attempted to acquire the trappings of the established elite in Beijing, and this included snuff bottles of all materials. Enamel on copper bottles provided the elevation in status that the *nouveau riche* demanded. Snuff bottles were perceived as a luxury item, being produced concurrently in the Palace Workshops for the emperor, his family, and his courtiers. They were also "foreign" and, therefore, sophisticated, as the skill of enameling had been partially developed by the Jesuits at court, and because the innovative subject matter of European pastoral scenes was often depicted upon them.

Between the Kangxi and Jiaqing reigns, at least twenty painters were transferred from Guangzhou to the Palace Workshops. They had to undertake tests to qualify for working, in often unpleasant conditions, and for a meager stipend. If successful, however, the craftsmen could become "Senior Painters." This meant that not only was their long-term future secure as enamellers but also that the emperors would give financial rewards to the best artists. It is documented that the Qianlong Emperor ordered six Canton enamellers to each produce an enamel on copper bottle as a test before they were accepted into the Palace Workshops. It is not recorded if all six were admitted!

One of the results of this was the transfer of style between Guangzhou and Beijing out of the palace and into the commercial mainstream. There may even have been an imperial copper workshop based in Guangzhou. Although no documentation exists for this, in the eighteenth century, the Qianlong Emperor had set up jade workshops around the country to supply him with jade pieces, and he may have set up other types of workshops in specific areas, such as Guangzhou. The manufacture of enamel on metal bottles in Guangzhou, specifically for the palace, appears to have strengthened the influence that Beijing had on the Guangzhou enamellers. Thus, throughout the Qianlong period, artists from Guangzhou were producing a range of enamel on metal objects, capable of equaling perhaps not the best of the Palace Workshops, but certainly as good as the mid-range output from there.

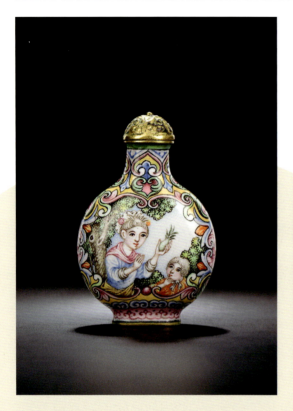
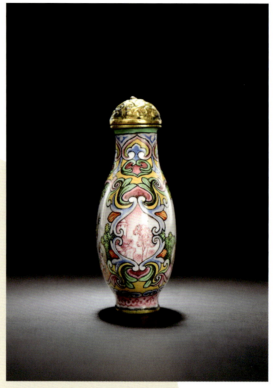

10

清乾隆　畫琺瑯西洋人物圖鼻煙壺

鼻煙壺金屬胎。直口，短頸，溜肩，腹微鼓，至中心點以下漸收，橢圓形圈足。壺口與圈足皆飾以鎏金，通體以畫琺瑯技法繪飾西洋人物。腹壁兩面與左右兩側，利用捲草紋勾勒，形成四個兩兩相對的花式開光，前後兩開光除人物位置左右相反，布局基本雷同，皆以一側的綠樹襯托遠景，近景則有一對母女持果凝望。又兩肩部的側邊開光內，猶以胭脂紅淡彩繪製迷濛的樓閣，開光外滿飾黃地如意雲肩紋錦地，近底足處並飾有一圈二方連續的藍彩如意雲紋與胭脂紅幾何紋。底部圈足內署藍釉「乾隆年製」兩行四字楷書款。

是類金屬胎畫琺瑯西洋人物，用色鮮麗明快，人物表情勾勒生動傳神，是乾隆朝吸取西洋透視畫法的別樣藝術成就。類似器今存兩岸故宮仍有諸多案例可資比對，詳見：李久芳主編《鼻煙壺》，商務印書館(香港) 有限公司，2003年，109-117頁。

1736-1795年
高：4.9 厘米

著錄：Bob C. Stevens, The Collector's Book of Snuff Bottles，紐約: John Weatherhill, Inc.，1976年，編號 980。

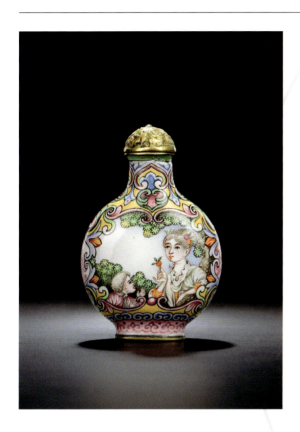

An enamel on copper with gold bottle, of flattened, rounded form with a cylindrical neck and a gilded mouth, with a gilt oval foot; decorated using *famille-rose* enamels within a scrolling vignette on each main side, one side with a portrait of a European woman dressed in flowing robes and with a garland of flowers in her hair, seated under a tree and holding out a fruit to a boy, the reverse with a similar scene with a European lady in formal attire with upswept hair holding up a fruit in front of a young boy; the two narrow sides decorated in pink enamel each within a scrolling vignette with a landscape of European buildings and trees; all surrounded with scrolling floral borders, a formal floral band above the foot and a band of *lingzhi* around the neck; the white enamel base with a blue enamel four-character *Qianlong nian zhi* mark in regular script, and of the period.

Imperial, attributed to the Palace Workshops, Beijing.

1736-1795
Height: 4.9 cm

Published: Bob C. Stevens, *The Collector's Book of Snuff Bottles*, New York: John Weatherhill, Inc.,1976, no. 980.

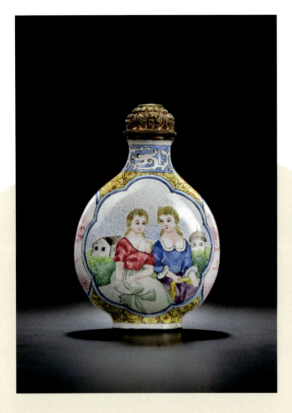 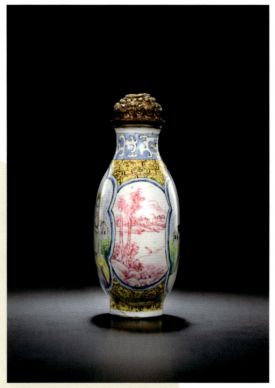

11

清乾隆　畫琺瑯西洋仕女圖鼻煙壺

金屬胎鼻煙壺，畫琺瑯裝飾技法與前述作品雷同。敞口、短頸微束，溜肩，扁圓腹，腹下漸收，橢圓形圈足。腹壁兩面做圓形八連弧開光，開光內飾西洋仕女，背後襯以鄉村小屋。仕女抵肩並坐，棕髮捲曲，服色鮮麗光彩且對比強烈，形塑濃郁的典雅歐式風韻。肩部兩側亦有束腰橢圓形開光，開光內以胭脂紅彩填繪中式山水小景，明顯營造中西合璧的藝術趣味。開光之外，通體滿飾黃釉龜背紋錦地，頸部一圈藍地變形夔紋寬帶，底部圈足內署藍彩「乾隆年製」兩行四字楷書款。

1736-1795年
高：5 厘米

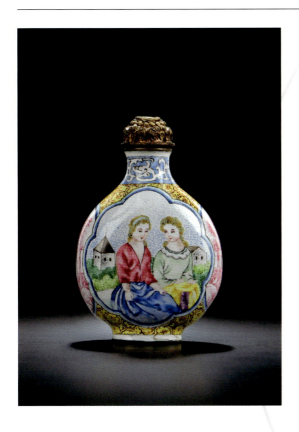

An enamel on copper bottle, of flattened, rounded form with a cylindrical neck and a gilded everted mouth, with a gilt oval foot; decorated using *famille-rose* enamels within a scrolling vignette on each main side, one side with a portrait of two demure European women dressed in flowing robes seated together and conversing, with European buildings and foliage behind them, the reverse with a similar scene with European women in *dishabille*; the two narrow sides decorated in pink enamel, each within a scrolling vignette with a landscape of a fisherman on a river with, on one bank, European buildings and on the other trees and rockwork; the connecting panels surrounded with formal floral borders, a formal scrolling band of archaic dragons around the neck; the white enamel base with a blue enamel four-character *Qianlong nian zhi* mark in regular script, and of the period.

Imperial, attributed to Guangzhou.

1736-1795
Height: 5 cm

12

清乾隆　畫琺瑯西洋莊園人物圖鼻煙壺

金屬胎鼻煙壺，呈扁瓶形，造型與裝飾亦略與前述作品雷同。腹壁兩面彩繪通景式莊園人物，一面遠山湖水迷濛，綠樹渚岸旁山羊回首跪臥，兩人物蹲踞其側，情態寧靜祥和。另一面莊園矗立遠方，湖水緩波，花草茂盛，一長髮女子垂足坐於湖石上，做拭汗休憩狀，而身後山羊翹首凝望遠方，似於靜默中完美傳達了溫煦旖旎的田園風光。底部圈足內署藍彩「乾隆年製」兩行四字楷書款。

是件鼻煙壺，用彩多樣而不失柔和，畫面運用西洋透視構圖，景物深遠，頗具立體感。又前後兩畫面既各自獨立，又相互融融於莊園景色而沒有一絲違和感，充分展現乾隆朝造辦處畫琺瑯的高超藝術造詣。

1736-1795年
高：4.6 厘米

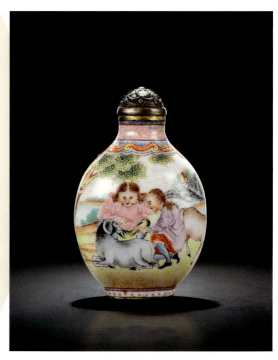

An enamel on copper bottle, of flattened, rounded form with a cylindrical neck and a gilded slightly everted mouth, with a gilt oval foot; decorated using *famille-rose* enamels with a continuous pastoral scene of two European children tending to sheep and a European woman dressed in flowing robes seated on a rock, with a landscape of a river and European buildings and foliage behind them; a formal scrolling band around the neck in pink enamel; the base with a band of pink enamel dots; the white enamel base with a blue enamel four-character *Qianlong nian zhi* mark in regular script, and of the period.

Imperial, attributed to Guangzhou.

1736-1795
Height: 4.6 cm

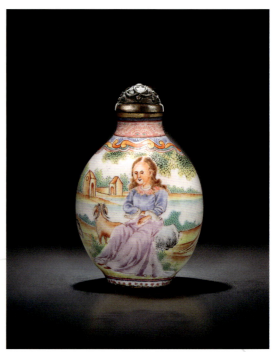

宮廷玻璃

料器在中國備受關注，康熙三十五年，即1696年，造辦處成立宮廷玻璃廠。從此，清代生產了大量的料器，其中包括鼻煙壺。最初從廣州、後從博山挑選工匠到北京宮廷作坊工作。1728年《養心殿造辦處史料輯覽》中提及在宮廷出現了廣東料胎所製的鼻煙壺。

十八世紀，料器經歷了由盛而衰，側面反映了清朝皇帝的命運。乾隆時期料器的品質達到頂峰，嘉慶年間相對停滯，從道光開始下降，這亦吻合當時的經濟發展。

宮廷玻璃廠最初建於紫禁城內。雍正年間遷往圓明園，直至清朝滅亡。我們需要謹記，十八世紀，北京與廣州、博山的工匠相互交流從無間斷。雖然這些工匠帶來了他們在宮外所學的工藝與知識，但在養心殿宮廷作坊中，他們必須服從宮內規制。宮廷作坊生產的作品，特別在紋飾與器形的選擇上十分明顯，如經典的仿青銅器與高古瓷紋飾的鼻煙壺作品。

在宮廷任職時，這些工匠得到洋人，特別得到在宮內輔助的傳教士指導。德裔傳教士紀利安按康熙皇帝旨意負責監督玻璃廠的建造。但傳教士們最大的貢獻是建造了大型的爐用於製作圓明園所需的花窗玻璃。1749-1753年，正值乾隆年間，製作玻璃的配方有所改變，石英、銅、鐵被大量的硼砂和砷所替代。這個改變應該和宮內傳教士有關。乾隆時期的傳世品顯示，博山當地的料器與北京所製以及宮廷作坊所製的料器成分相似。

一些清早期料器表面有細裂紋。最初被認為是源於其配方中鹼性物質的比例失衡，是工藝上的瑕疵。現在我們知道這是因為把西洋玻璃的碎片加入配方所造成的。當時廣州的工匠認為這樣可以極大的提高玻璃的淨度。當然，慢慢地他們發現這反而導致料器表面產生細裂紋。在十八世紀上半葉，將西洋玻璃熔入中國料器製作的現象大約持續了近三十年。

清早期康熙與雍正年間，料器製作高速發展，工匠們創造了各種顏色。當時有透明、白色、半透明藍色、黃色以及最被推崇的紅色（內含膠體狀金）。

清代最重要的顏色之一是黃色，黃色的使用嚴格受到皇家禮儀制度規範，僅供皇室成員使用。雍正皇帝偏好檸檬黃，乾隆皇帝則喜好明黃。但這種規制自嘉慶年間逐漸瓦解。由於腐敗以及國力漸弱，道光皇帝甚至向非貴族的富商出售使用黃色的權力以換取金錢填充國庫。

在造辦處玻璃廠創建初期，流行金星玻璃。這是一種滿佈金色斑點的玻璃。初創於乾隆時期鼻煙壺，在滿佈金色斑點的褐紅色玻璃前後加夾透明玻璃層而成。看似簡單的玻璃素器，實為一個反映當時高超工藝的精品。

乾隆時期，料器產量增加，顏色的類別與深淺也多種多樣，十八世紀中，還創作出橄欖綠、不透明孔雀藍、紫等色。雖然沿用前人技藝，但此時工藝日臻精細。

除了單色料器，單色套料及多色套料的工藝亦日趨成熟。發展出多種顏色的套料，包括有藍、綠、黃、紫、黑以及最常見的寶石紅。同時，不僅有透明地、白地及雪花地，色地選擇也逐漸增加。

當時精湛的玻璃工藝可以生產出繁複而自然的套色效果與裝飾紋樣，其中有融合西洋與中國工藝的作品。

因此，這時期的裝飾，在吹製器皿上運用了雕刻、暗刻、砂輪切割，描金及彩繪等工藝裝飾。器形與裝飾題材是當時文化規範的演變。當時的玻璃製造達到頂峰，但盛極必衰，隨著嘉慶、道光時期的經濟衰退，造辦處玻璃廠所製玻璃的數量和質量均有所下滑。宮廷不再需要大量的玻璃工匠，他們逐漸被遣返各地，繼續在宮外傳承玻璃製作。

GLASS

Interest in glass in China was such that in the 35th year of the reign of Kangxi, the imperial glasshouse was founded in 1696. From that time, and throughout the Qing dynasty, the glassworks turned out a great number of objects, including snuff bottles. Craftsmen were sent firstly from Guangzhou, and later from Boshan to the imperial Palace Workshops in Beijing. In 1728 the *Documents of Production of Yangxin Hall Palace Workshops* of the *Imperial Household Department of the Qing Dynasty* mentions the appearance at the court of 'snuff bottles of the Qing Guangzhou glass.'

During the eighteenth century, the glassworks went from prosperity to decline, reflecting the fortunes of the Qing emperors. It reached its peak of top quality production during the Qianlong period, lay relatively idle during the Jiaqing era, and started to decline from Daoguang onwards, reflecting in part the economic climate of those times.

The imperial glasshouse was built within the confines of the Forbidden City. During the reign of Yongzheng, it was moved to the Summer Palace, the Yuanming Yuan, where it remained until the end of the Qing dynasty. It is important to remember that continually throughout the eighteenth century there was a cross-fertilization of ideas due to the movement of workers to Beijing from Boshan and Guangzhou. Whilst these workers brought with them the techniques and knowledge acquired outside the palace, at the imperial workshops, Yangxin Hall, they were artistically subjected to the restrictions imposed by the court. This manifests itself predominantly in the choice of subject matter, and shape, with the Palace Workshops producing wares including snuff bottles with the classical archaistic designs seen on bronzes and ceramics.

Whilst working at the palace, the craftsmen were aided by Westerners, and specifically the Jesuit missionaries who were seconded to the court. It was a German missionary, Kilian Stumpff who was ordered by the Kangxi Emperor to construct the first imperial glasshouse. However, the Jesuit's main contribution appears to be in the building of larger furnaces to produce bigger items such as window panes for the Yuanming Yuan. From 1740-1753, during the Qianlong period, the recipe for glass changed somewhat; quartz, copper, and iron were dropped from the mixture, whilst borax and arsenic were added in high quantities. This change seems to be directly related to the presence of the Jesuits at court. The remainder of the Qianlong period shows a similarity in composition between glass produced in Boshan and that attributed to Beijing and the imperial factory.

Some early Qing dynasty glass exhibits a phenomenon known as 'crizzling.' It was originally thought that this was merely a bad recipe in the glass with the alkaline content being disproportionate to the mix. However, it is now known that crizzling was caused by the introduction of foreign crushed Western glass into the mix. This was unwittingly done by the craftsmen from Guangzhou in the belief that they were creating a stronger glass with greater clarity. Over time, of course, the opposite has proved true as the virus of crizzling has taken hold over these pieces. Foreign glass was combined with Chinese glass for about three decades during the first half of the eighteenth century.

During the early years of Qing dynasty glass production, in the reigns of Kangxi and Yongzheng, new colors were quickly added to the repertoire of the glassmakers. Clear glass, white, translucent blue, yellow, and a highly appreciated red (which contained colloidal gold) were the order of the day.

One of the important colors in the Qing period was opaque yellow as it was the color bound by imperial regulations and restricted in its usage to members of the imperial family. Whilst the Yongzheng Emperor preferred a more lemon-yellow tone, the Qianlong Emperor favored a bright clear yellow. Such regulations fell apart from the Jiaqing period onwards. The corrupt, and increasingly poorer, Daoguang Emperor even sold the right to use yellow to the less aristocratic, but wealthy merchant classes to raise cash for the imperial coffers.

From the early days of the imperial glasshouse, there was an interest in what we today call aventurine glass. This is glass interspersed with gold flecking. This developed in the Qianlong period with snuff bottles made of reddish-brown glass which is interspersed with gold flecks and sandwiched between two layers of transparent glass. What at first appears as a fairly simple plain piece of glass is in reality a sophisticated example of established manufacture.

During the Qianlong period, the output was prolific with a myriad of additional colors and tones such as olive green, opaque turquoise, and purple being added to the eighteenth-century palette. Techniques became increasingly sophisticated though they followed the tradition of the previous reigns.

Aligned with this advanced stage of development of monochromes were the fine overlay glass pieces of both single and multiple casing. The breadth of overlay colors increased dramatically to include blue, green, yellow, purple, black as well as the more common ruby-red. Not content with overlaying glass onto a plain, white, or snowflake ground the variation in background color also increased.

A now highly versatile glass industry could produce complex and seemingly spontaneous combinations of colors and designs, some of which were European in influence and Chinese in technique.

Decoration during this time, therefore, involved techniques of carving, incising, wheel-cutting, gilding, and enameling onto pieces that were mostly mold-blown. Form and subject matter was an evolution of existing cultural norms. Glassmaking at this time had reached its zenith, but what goes up must come down, and as the fortunes of the Jiaqing and Daoguang emperors diminished, so too did the quality and quantity of glass produced in the imperial glasshouse. As fewer workers were needed there, they returned from whence they had come continuing the tradition of glass manufacture away from the court.

13

清　黃玻璃刻幾何獸面紋鼻煙壺

黃色玻璃，呈雞油黃。直口，短頸，溜肩，扁圓腹，腹下漸收，圈足。通體浮雕典雅的幾何獸面紋，由上至下分別是：頸部兩道二方連續彎弧紋，肩部鐫夔龍紋，腹部浮雕幾何獸面紋，近底足處則飾以變形蕉葉紋。又兩側面亦分別有上牛首、下雙立足鳥紋的圖樣。全器意象豐富，妝點工整，層次分別，能在單一色彩中追求繁複的視覺變化，誠屬難能可貴也。

1730-1770年
高：4.6 厘米

A glass bottle, of flattened, rounded form, with shoulders sloping to a cylindrical neck and with a wide mouth, with a neatly carved oval footrim; of translucent opaque yellow tone; carved with a continuous formal archaistic design of four animal heads; the narrow sides with archaistic birds; between a petal lappet band around the foot and two further similar bands around the neck.

Imperial, attributed to the Palace Workshops, Beijing.

1730-1770
Height: 4.6 cm

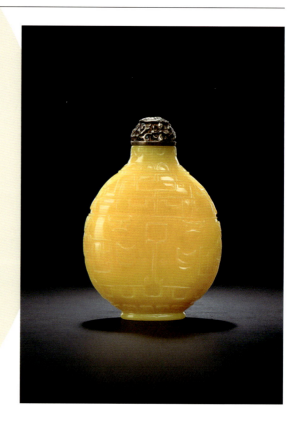

14

清　金星玻璃罐形鼻煙壺

金星玻璃，通體隱隱有金星閃閃。呈罐形。直口，短頸，折肩，菊瓣式長深腹，腹下漸收，底足微內凹。頸部套有金屬可掀式活帽蓋，帽蓋打開後，猶配有蓮瓣式圓蓋，形成蓋中有蓋的別樣洞天。

是件鼻煙壺基本光素，以二方連續菊瓣形帶起美妙的視覺變化，再加上獨特的蓋帽設計，乃至金星玻璃的存世量相對稀少等因素，故顯彌足珍貴。

1730-1770年
高：4 厘米

A glass bottle, of small, octagonal baluster form with a wide cylindrical neck with concave panels running vertically to the deep circular concave foot; the neck with a ridged bronze collar attaching the main body to the cover, which hides the stopper; the material of vivid, aventurine glass.

Imperial, attributed to the Palace Workshops, Beijing.

1730-1770
Height: 4 cm

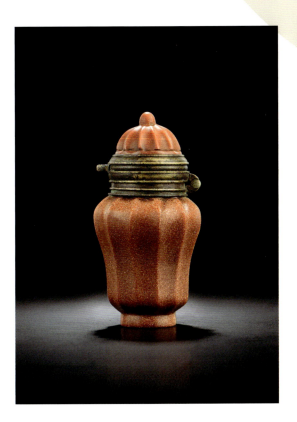

15

清乾隆　雄黃色玻璃磨稜鼻煙壺

鼻煙壺直口，短頸，圓鼓深腹，圈足。通體渾圓飽滿，以攪色玻璃工藝製成，呈雄黃色。又腹壁磨切成規則的六邊形連續，形成六角幾何形律動與攪色不規則斑紋相互交錯的豐富視覺效果，是一件具有抽象思維的掌中佳器。底部鐫「乾隆年製」兩行四字陰刻楷書款。

1736-1770年
高：5.3 厘米

A glass bottle, of rounded bulbous form with a cylindrical neck and a flat foot, the surface continuously carved with multi-faceted hexagons; the material of vivid swirling orange tones in imitation of realgar; the base with a wheel-cut four-character *Qianlong nian zhi* mark in regular script, and of the period.

Imperial, attributed to the Palace Workshops, Beijing.

1736-1770
Height: 5.3 cm

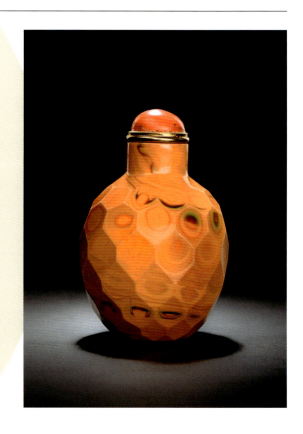

16

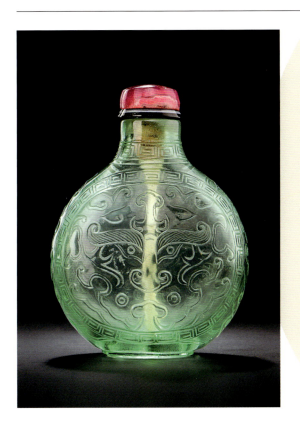

清　透明綠色玻璃獸面紋鼻煙壺

透明綠色玻璃。直口，溜肩，扁圓腹，腹下漸收，橢圓形圈
足。頸部近肩處，飾一匝二方連續方雷紋，腹壁兩面以方雷紋
框，圍成圓形開光，開光內浮雕獸面紋，正面獸面近似牛首，
兩邊圍繞相向而視的雙螭龍。壺體兩側刻上下二方連續的如意
雲肩紋，中心點飾以圓形寶珠。全器雕工典雅，造型飽滿，具
有鮮明的皇家裝飾特色。

1750-1800年
高：6.3 厘米

A glass bottle, of flattened, rounded form, with shoulders
sloping to a cylindrical neck and with a wide mouth,
with a neatly carved oval footrim; of translucent green
tone; carved on each main side with a formal archaistic
design of a *taotie* mask within a circular vignette bordered
by a *leiwen* pattern, a similar band encircling the neck.

Probably Imperial, attributed to the Palace Workshops,
Beijing.

1750-1800
Height: 6.3 cm

17

清　透明玻璃海水藍「福祿萬代」鼻煙壺

透明玻璃呈海水藍。敞口，短頸，溜肩，扁圓腹，腹下漸收，
橢圓形圈足。腹壁兩面以琢玉技法淺浮雕纏枝葫蘆，葫蘆自然
垂盪搖曳，藤蔓葳蕤，生機益然，其間並有蝙蝠盤飛，可謂完
美傳達了「福祿萬代」的吉祥寓意。

是件鼻煙壺胎體厚實，玻璃顏色如寶石般夢幻，尤其是工藝精
湛的典麗雕工，誠然讓人愛不釋手。

1750-1800年
高：6 厘米

A glass bottle, of flattened, rounded form, with shoulders
sloping to a cylindrical neck and with a wide mouth,
with a neatly carved oval footrim; of translucent
emerald-green tone; carved with a continuous design of
bats flying amongst leafy double gourds.

Imperial, attributed to the Palace Workshops, Beijing.

1750-1800
Height: 6 cm

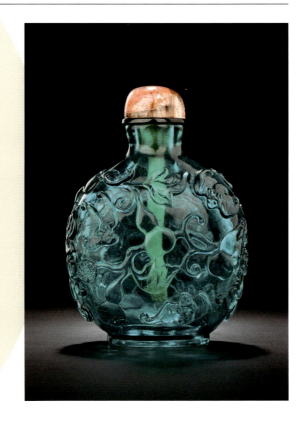

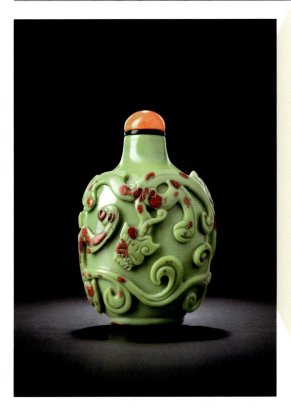

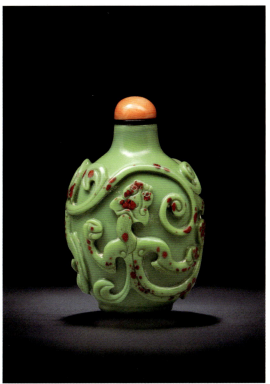

18

清　綠色玻璃灑朱斑蟠螭紋鼻煙壺

鼻煙壺直口，溜肩，扁圓腹，腹下漸收，橢圓形圈足，圈足滿布朱色斑點。通體以綠色不透明玻璃為地，上攬不規則朱色斑點，腹壁利用剔地技法，浮雕呈上下相倚的二蟠螭。蟠螭身軀修長，捲曲盤繞，線條流暢優美。此外，因剔地技法的巧妙搭配，讓朱色斑點只點綴於螭龍身軀，對比綠色玻璃地的單一致爽，實有畫龍點睛的藝術效果。

1750-1800年
高：5 厘米

A glass bottle, of slightly bulbous, ovoid form, with shoulders sloping to a cylindrical neck, with a neatly carved oval footrim; of opaque celadon-green tone with dark red inclusions; carved with a continuous design of coiling *chilong*.

Imperial, attributed to the Palace Workshops, Beijing.

1750-1800
Height: 5 cm

19

清　寶石紅玻璃夔鳳紋鼻煙壺

鼻煙壺作扁瓶形。直口，削肩，垂腹，橢圓形圈足。通體透明
寶石紅色玻璃刻花，頸肩部飾一圈陰刻蕉葉紋，腹部兩面浮雕
呈首、尾、足相抵的夔鳳紋。肩部兩側浮雕一束如意捲草紋，
表徵「一生如意」的吉祥寓意。本件鼻煙壺的玻璃呈色清透深
邃，寶石紅的濃郁如幻似真，所琢夔鳳紋組構規矩，典雅精
緻，能臻宮廷造辦處的皇家造詣水平。

1730-1795年
高：6.8 厘米

A glass bottle, of flattened, elongated, ovoid form, with
shoulders sloping to a cylindrical neck, with a wide
mouth, and with a neatly carved oval footrim; of vivid
ruby-red tone; carved on each main side with a pair of
formalized, archaistic confronting dragons beside raised
bosses; the narrow sides carved with tied scrolls in *ruyi*
form; below a border of acanthus leaves around the neck.

Imperial, attributed to the Palace Workshops, Beijing.

1730-1795
Height: 6.8 cm

20

清　寶石紅玻璃弦紋鼻煙壺

玻璃鼻煙壺呈透明寶石紅色。作扁瓶形。直口，削肩，垂腹，橢圓形圈足。通體雕飾微波浪起伏的凸弦紋，凸弦紋自頸肩處由短到長，至腹部中心點又由長到短，充分展現律動曼妙的秩序感。

是件鼻煙壺造形清癯扁瘦，然諦視凸弦紋回還往復的重複視覺印象，又添視豐富的無窮韻律，是一件具有簡約風尚的清雅藝術珍品。

1750-1795年
高：6.6 厘米

A glass bottle, of slender, elongated ovoid form; of clear ruby-red tone; carved horizontally with ribbed, wavy bands from the cylindrical neck, with wide mouth, to the oval footrim.

Imperial, attributed to the Palace Workshops, Beijing.

1750-1795
Height: 6.6 cm

21

清　粉紅色玻璃蓮瓣紋鼻煙壺

鼻煙壺呈扁瓶形。敞口，短頸，溜肩，腹下漸收，圈足。通體
粉紅色玻璃，利用吹製與琢玉技法，滿飾層層疊壓的蓮瓣紋。
底部圈足以莖梗紋圍繞而成，中間並飾有蒂頭。圈足之上琢刻
向上捲覆的蓮荷，四邊荷葉並向外翻捲。荷葉之上做三層前後
疊壓的蓮瓣，蓮瓣飽滿寫實，展現自然生機。全器雕工精湛，
像一朵綻放的蓮花，訴說無上清境的人間淨土。

1750-1795年
高：5.5 厘米

A glass bottle, of rounded form, with a cylindrical neck
and slightly everted mouth, and with a neatly carved oval
foot; the opaque pale pink and white glass continuously
carved with overlapping lotus petals enfolded towards the
base by a curling lotus leaf.

Imperial, attributed to the Palace Workshops, Beijing.

1750-1795
Height: 5.5 cm

22

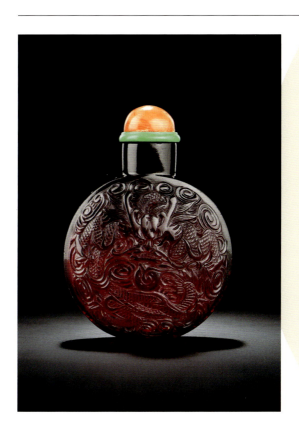

清　暗紅色玻璃團龍紋鼻煙壺

鼻煙壺呈扁瓶形。直口，短頸，扁圓腹，平底。通體半透明紅色玻璃，頸壁與兩側壁光素無紋。前後兩腹壁構圖雷同，皆做正面團龍紋，龍頭飾雙角，頷鬚長鬍，張口露齒，形象威猛。四周襯以捲雲紋，表徵祥龍騰躍於雲際之間的九五尊貴氣息。

是件鼻煙壺飾有紋樣的腹壁，其構圖布局幾乎是密不通風，然兩側邊卻又一任光素，仔細推敲，這一密一疏之間，正發揮了視覺平衡的高度統一，其高超的美學造詣委實令人激賞。

1750-1820年
高：5.2 厘米

A glass bottle, of flattened, rounded form, with a cylindrical neck; of dark ruby-red tone; carved on each main side with a coiling scaly dragon in pursuit of a flaming pearl, flying through scrolling clouds which frame the scene; with flattened narrow sides.

Imperial, attributed to the Palace Workshops, Beijing.

1750-1820
Height: 5.2 cm

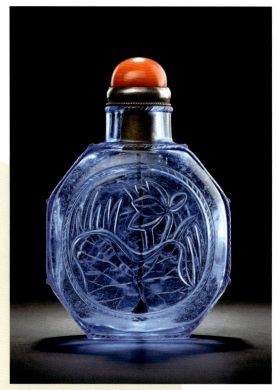

23

清乾隆　海水藍玻璃「一品清廉」鼻煙壺

鼻煙壺呈八角扁瓶形。唇口，斜削肩，八角扁圓腹，繭形凹底。通體透明海水藍玻璃，壺口與壺身邊緣皆飾以凸起的繩紋，腹壁兩面亦以凸繩紋圍成圓形開光，開光內一面淺浮雕荷葉青蓮，表徵「一品清廉」；另一面則飾水草鯰魚，寓意「年年有餘」，底部鐫「乾隆年製」兩行四字楷書款。全器雕工細膩，紋樣討喜，應是出自宮廷造辦處的箇中精品。

1750-1795年
高：6.4 厘米

A glass bottle, of octagonal faceted form, with a cylindrical neck and a neatly carved flat oval foot, each main side with a circular panel; of clear sapphire-blue tone; one side carved with a fan-tailed carp swimming in a pond beside aquatic weeds, the reverse with lotus leaves, flowers and pods; the circular panel, the neck and the outer edges of the facets all carved with rope-twist edges; the base with a wheel-cut four-character *Qianlong nian zhi* mark in regular script, and of the period.

Imperial, attributed to the Palace Workshops, Beijing.

1750-1795
Height: 6.4 cm

24

清道光　天藍色玻璃磨稜八角鼻煙壺

鼻煙壺呈八角扁瓶形。直口，斜削肩，八角扁圓腹，側壁磨成委角，平底。通體不透明天藍色玻璃，全器一任光素，唯於腹部凸起圓形開光，開光內磨切成四斜坡幾何形，中心點錐凸高起。底部陰刻「道光年製」兩行四字楷書款。

是件鼻煙壺胎體厚實，用料講究，磨製精湛，是道光朝宮廷造辦處的典型佳器。

1821-1850年
高：5.5 厘米

A glass bottle, of octagonal faceted form with raised panels on the front and reverse, carved as diagonally segmented quatrefoils, with a cylindrical neck and a neatly carved flat oval foot; of opaque turquoise tone; the base with a wheel-cut four-character *Daoguang nian zhi* mark in regular script, and of the period.

Imperial, attributed to the Palace Workshops, Beijing.

1821-1850
Height: 5.5 cm

25

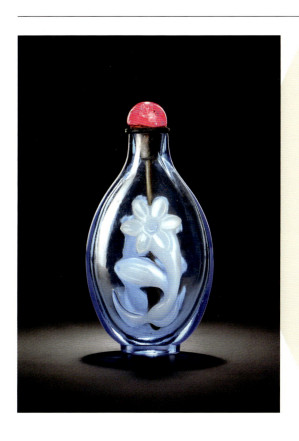

清　海水藍套白玻璃折枝花卉鼻煙壺

鼻煙壺呈扁瓶形。直口，短頸，溜肩，扁圓腹，腹下漸收，圈足。通體以透明海水藍為地，腹壁兩面套白色玻璃，並以剔地技法高浮雕折枝梔子花。全器水藍地白色顯花，但由於海水藍地的水漾穿透效果，遂讓梔子花予人一種漂浮的視覺夢幻。

1736-1795年
高：5.9 厘米

A glass bottle, of flattened ovoid form tapering to a slender neck, and with a neatly carved oval footrim; overlaid with opaque white on a clear sapphire-blue ground; carved on the front and reverse with a flowering gentian and a single closed bud.

Imperial, attributed to the Palace Workshops, Beijing.

1736-1795
Height: 5.9 cm

26

清　藍地套白色玻璃凌霄花鼻煙壺

鼻煙壺呈扁瓶形。直口，短頸，溜肩，扁深腹，橢圓形圈足。
通體半透明寶藍地套白色玻璃，腹壁兩面以剔地技法，高浮雕
六朵折枝凌霄花，一面做飾四朵，另一面安二朵，花卉開合交
錯各有不同，營造豐富的視覺效果。底部圈足亦套飾一圈白色
玻璃，恰與白色顯花完美呼應，可稱神來之添彩妙趣。

1736-1795年
高：5.8 厘米

A glass bottle, of flattened rectangular form with
shoulders tapering to a cylindrical neck, and with a
neatly carved oval footrim; overlaid with opaque white
on a vivid cobalt-blue ground; carved on the front and
reverse with a pair of overlapping flowering gentians.

Imperial, attributed to the Palace Workshops, Beijing.

1736-1795
Height: 5.8 cm

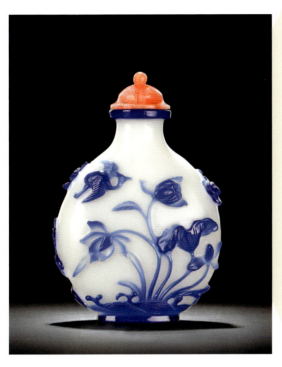

清　白地套藍玻璃「一品清廉」鼻煙壺

扁瓶形鼻煙壺。唇口，短頸，溜肩，扁圓腹，腹下漸收，橢圓
形圈足。通體白地套藍玻璃，腹壁兩面以琢玉技法，一面浮雕
挺勁的蓮荷，蓮荷之上有飛鶴凌空，表徵「一品清廉」之意；
另一面浮雕湖石牡丹，牡丹朵花綻放，搖曳生姿，寓意「富貴
長壽」。全器構圖雋秀淡雅，紋樣裝飾寓意吉祥，誠然是十八
世紀典型精品。

1750-1795年
高：5.6 厘米

A glass bottle, of flattened, rounded form with shoulders
tapering to a cylindrical neck with slightly everted mouth
and with a neatly carved oval footrim; overlaid in blue on
a milk-white ground; carved on one side with flowering
peonies issuing from rockwork, the reverse with lotus
leaves, flowers and pods growing in a pond, with a crane
in flight above, the mouth of the bottle with a blue
glass collar.

Imperial, attributed to the Palace Workshops, Beijing.

1750-1795
Height: 5.6 cm

28

清乾隆　白地套藍玻璃團葵紋鼻煙壺

鼻煙壺扁瓶形。直口，短頸，溜肩，扁圓腹，腹下漸收，橢圓形圈足。通體白地套藍玻璃，腹壁兩面中心各浮雕一團葵紋，兩側肩飾束帶捲草紋，捲草紋至束帶處交錯，然後向上下四方延展，形成不同視角俱有不同構圖的美學趣味。全器裝飾風格簡約疏朗，用色明快高雅，予人愉悅的視覺感受。底部陰刻「乾隆年製」橫書四字篆體款。

1736-1795年
高：5.6 厘米

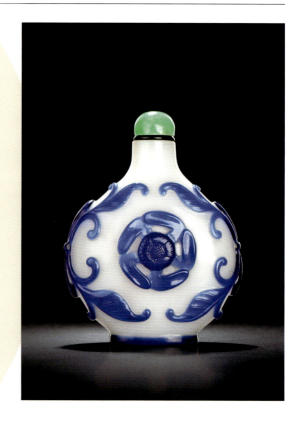

A glass bottle, of flattened, rounded form with shoulders tapering to a cylindrical neck and with a neatly carved oval footrim; overlaid in blue on a milk-white ground; carved on each main side with a central roundel of a mallow flower, the two narrow sides carved with a scrolling design depicting a tied bow and ribbon; the base with an incised four-character *Qianlong nian zhi* mark in seal script, and of the period.

Imperial, attributed to the Palace Workshops, Beijing.

1736-1795
Height: 5.6 cm

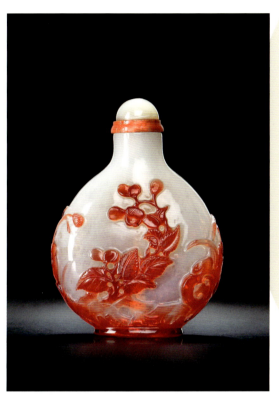

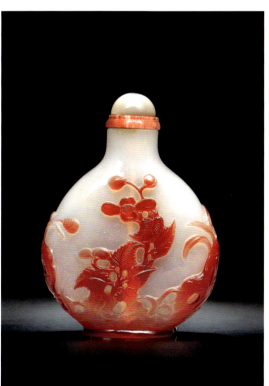

清　乳白地套紅玻璃海棠花卉鼻煙壺

鼻煙壺通體呈扁瓶形。直口，短頸，溜肩，扁圓腹，腹下漸
收，橢圓形圈足。白色半透明地套紅玻璃，全器近底足處飾以
一周嶙峋的湖石，腹壁兩面折枝海棠生於湖石間，兩肩側面則
叢蘭搖曳於聳立的怪石間。海棠朵花或含苞、或綻放，流露出
高雅的自然生機，亦隱隱有一種難以言詮的文人禪趣。

1750-1795年
高：5.7 厘米

A glass bottle, of flattened, rounded form with shoulders
tapering to a cylindrical neck and with a neatly carved
oval footrim; overlaid in red on a translucent white
ground; carved on each main side with a leafy branch of
blossoming fruit beside grasses, issuing from rockwork.

Imperial, attributed to the Palace Workshops, Beijing.

1750-1795
Height: 5.7 cm

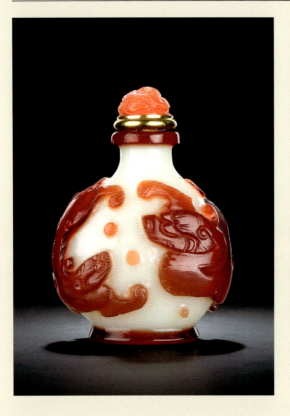
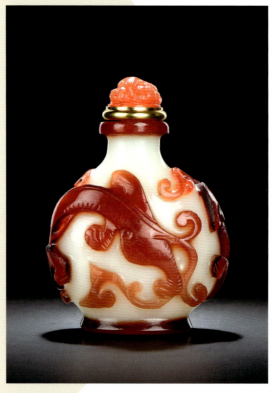

清乾隆　白地套紅玻璃雙螭戲珠鼻煙壺

鼻煙壺作扁瓶形。唇口，短頸，溜肩，扁圓腹，腹下漸收，橢圓形圈足。通體白套紅玻璃，腹壁以剔地技法，高浮雕雙螭龍，螭龍環繞於腹壁兩面，一上一下做相互追逐戲珠貌。螭龍身軀矯健，前肢厚實，惟線條流暢，形象生動，展現威猛且不失輕靈的舞動感。底部圈足套紅料，內署「乾隆年製」橫書陰刻楷體款。

1736-1795年
高：5.6 厘米

A glass bottle, of small, flattened, rounded form with shoulders tapering to a cylindrical neck and with a neatly carved, slightly splayed oval footrim; overlaid in red on a milk-white ground; continuously carved with raised bosses and a pair of dragons coiling around the bottle; the mouth of the bottle with a red glass collar; the base with an incised four-character *Qianlong nian zhi* mark in seal script, and of the period.

Imperial, attributed to the Palace Workshops, Beijing.

1736-1795
Height: 5.6 cm

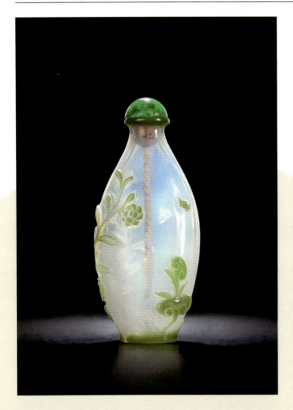

31

清　卵青地套淡綠色玻璃「福壽如意」鼻煙壺

鼻煙壺綠色。唇口，溜肩，深腹，腹下漸收，淡綠色圈足。全器卵青色地套淡綠色玻璃，腹壁利用浮雕技法，鐫飾折枝靈芝花卉，花卉之上並有蝙蝠與蝴蝶盤旋左右。從圖像寓意來看，蝙「蝠」諧音「福」，蝴蝶的「蝶」諧音「耋」，代表長壽，而靈芝花卉自有如意的意涵，縮合起來遂有「福壽如意」的吉祥意思。又構圖中靈芝草在卵青地的映襯下，宛如修草在水中搖曳飄盪，其視覺上的美好，也激盪出旖旎的浪漫韻致，很難不讓人拊掌稱好。

1750-1795年
高：5.7 厘米

A glass bottle, of slender, elongated, ovoid form with shoulders tapering to a cylindrical neck and with a neatly carved oval footrim; overlaid in pale green on a translucent white ground; continuously carved with flowering plants with butterflies flitting above, the mouth of the bottle with a green glass collar.

Imperial, attributed to the Palace Workshops, Beijing.

1750-1795
Height: 5.7 cm

宮廷玉

康熙、雍正年間，僅在紫禁城內設有一間製作玉器的作坊。作坊共聘請了二十五人，包括七名工匠，一名鑲嵌師以及十七名雕工。因為當時原料枯竭，他們主要負責修復前朝玉器珍品，直到1759年乾隆皇帝收復和闐地區，這個情況才有所改變。乾隆取得該區域管轄權後，每年下令開採和闐玉兩次，每次各兩噸，並運往紫禁城製作鼻煙壺等玉器珍玩。玉料自乾隆起供應穩定，直至嘉慶1821年終斷。

十八世紀，造辦處下設多個作坊，其中玉器作坊不僅設於紫禁城內，亦遍佈全國。為了滿足自身對玉器的喜好，乾隆皇帝下旨在京外設立八處玉器作坊作為內廷玉作的補充。除了天津，其他七處均在南方：鳳陽、杭州、淮安、江寧、九江、蘇州以及揚州。

這些宮廷玉器作坊，特別是內廷玉作所製的玉雕鼻煙壺特徵鮮明。值得注意的是它們尺寸相對較小，眾多例子顯示，內廷所製的鼻煙壺小於宮外所製。這不僅限於玉質鼻煙壺，京城內廷所製銅胎畫琺瑯鼻煙壺與料胎鼻煙壺亦相對小巧。

另一個御製玉鼻煙壺的特徵是直頸，與口沿相接，就像一個完整的領口。這種頸部設計，其口沿一般較寬。對於料胎鼻煙壺來說，直頸寬口是吸引人的特徵，因為它反映了當時可以成熟掌控玻璃吹製工藝，但對於玉鼻煙壺，這種設計讓工匠較容易進行掏膛。宮廷作坊的工匠可以把玉鼻煙壺的壺身掏得如紙一樣薄，但這不是必要要求。合理的鼻煙壺掏膛比例，壺身下方五分之一處較厚實，以增加其整體重量，使其達到平衡和穩固。其次，有記載表明有些情況下會連夜放置乾花於壺嘴，給壺中的鼻煙添香。較大的壺口，亦使得這個程式更容易。

乾隆皇帝鍾愛玉器，特別鍾情前朝流傳下來的古玉。乾隆後期，隨著玉石原料供應充足，乾隆皇帝下旨大量製作玉雕。這些玉器分由全國八處宮廷作坊所製。當時，在製作過程中進行染色處理是為了追求古意，模仿古玉的質感與皮。乾隆八年，當乾隆皇帝看到呈獻上來，由皇家作坊製作的兩件白玉小件，他下旨：「首領薩木哈來說，太監胡世傑、張玉交古圖一套。傳旨將做來白人，玉馬，照考古圖內顏色燒造。欽此。」旨意本身十分有意思，它表明了皇帝對玉器生產相當重視，並瞭解其整個生產過程。

本收藏有一例十八世紀御製白玉磨棱八方形鼻煙壺，十分稀有，這器形源於歐洲，常見於玻璃器皿，亦見同類石英器皿。在歐洲，使用多方形可以展示切割後寶石的光彩，如紅寶石。但造辦處使用這個器形僅因其新奇，在宮廷屬創新器形。採用多方形設計，料胎鼻煙壺可通過各面折射，凸顯材料本身的光彩，但白玉並不透明，即使內腔工藝完美，也無法達到這種效果。

葫蘆寓意長壽，因其內含大量種子，亦有多子多孫之意。作為裝飾主題，葫蘆常見於各種材料所製的鼻煙壺上，如玉、瓷、料等。也有以葫蘆為器形，更有直接由葫蘆所製的作品。人們還賦予了葫蘆其他寓意，他們認為，葫蘆上腹部象徵天，即人們所嚮往的天國；葫蘆下腹部象徵地，即人們所生活的人間。即使在宮廷，葫蘆寓意的重要性無法被低估。清內務府造辦處檔案總滙記載，1754年，匣裱作遵旨為一件綠地套藍料葫蘆形花瓶製作箱匣。檔案中特意標明此件花瓶將存放於宮內，而非用於賞賜，顯示其備受珍視。

翡翠

一直以來，中國人十分喜愛翡翠。這種礦石在明末已為人所知，但直到乾隆晚期，翡翠被宮廷作為傳統玉石的替代材料，才被視作一種珍貴材料。翡翠大約在十八世紀末開始被開採。它硬度比傳統玉石高，卻易碎，因此雕刻難度高。淨度高的帝王綠翡翠很少用於製作鼻煙壺，蘋果綠翡翠則更常見。翡翠的魅力使其迅速成為乾隆皇帝以及其他宗室所鍾愛的材料。

JADE

During the Kangxi and Yongzheng periods, only one jade workshop existed within the palace confines. It employed twenty-five workers, of whom seven were craftsmen, one an inlayer, and seventeen carvers. These workers mostly repaired and restored jade pieces from earlier dynasties since there was a dearth of fresh material available until the Qianlong Emperor conquered the area around Khotan in 1759. After Qianlong gained control of the territory, two tons of Khotan jade were mined twice a year and sent to the palace to be fashioned into carvings, which included snuff bottles. The supply lasted through the remainder of the Qianlong period and into the subsequent Jiaqing period, until 1820 when the era came to an end.

The imperial workshops were well established by the eighteenth century, with jade workshops not only within the palace but also around the country. The Qianlong Emperor, to satisfy his passion for jade wares, ordered the establishment of eight jade workshops, supplementing the one at the palace. Apart from Tianjin, the other seven locations were in Jiangsu province: Fengyang, Hangzhou, Huaian, Jiangning, Jiujiang, Suzhou, and Yangzhou.

Jade snuff bottles produced in the imperial workshops, and specifically within the imperial palace have certain recognizable characteristics. The small size of the bottles is worth noting, as many examples with a palace attribution are distinctly smaller than bottles produced outside the palace confines. This holds true not only for jade examples, but also for enamel on metal and glass bottles produced in the Beijing Palace Workshops.

Another feature of imperial jade bottles is a "straightened" neck as it approaches the mouth of the bottle, almost like an integral collar. One often finds such a neck in combination with a "wide" mouth. This is considered an appealing feature of glass bottles, as it demonstrates control of the glass-blowing process, but with jade bottles, it allows the carver to more easily hollow out the vessel. The paper-thin hollowing of jade bottles from the Palace Workshops does not, however, seem to be an essential requirement. While the bottles are usually reasonably hollowed, they frequently have a solid area in the bottom fifth of the bottle, presumably to weight the bottle, give it balance and stability. Additionally, it is recorded that dried flowers were sometimes placed in the mouth of bottles overnight to freshen and give fragrance to the snuff in the bottle. With a bottle that had a wide mouth, this would have been an easier task.

The Qianlong Emperor had a great fondness for jade and in particular for the archaic jade of preceding dynasties. In the second half of his reign when the supply of jade was more plentiful he ordered that a large number of pieces be made. These were manufactured by order in the eight workshops around the country. The point of staining jade at the time of manufacture was in keeping with the spirit of archaism by producing pieces that reflect the hue and patination of earlier pieces. In 1743 the Qianlong Emperor gave instructions for the improvement, as he saw it, of two white jade pieces which had been ordered from the imperial workshops eleven months earlier. His orders were:

'Bake the white jade Immortal and horse to create some stains so they look like Han jades, and make an elegant stand for each of them.'

In itself, this instruction is of great interest as it shows that the emperor had a direct interest and knowledge of the manufacturing process.

This collection houses an eighteenth-century imperial pure white jade bottle of octagonal faceted form, a rarity in any collection, its European-derived shape usually being found in glass and occasionally quartz. The intention of using faceting in Europe would have been, for example, to showcase the brilliance of a cut gemstone (such as a ruby), while this form in the imperial palace would have simply been seen as a novelty and an innovative shape at the court. While faceted glass bottles enhance the radiance of the material, an opaque-white jade bottle, however well hollowed, would not demonstrate the same effect.

Double gourds symbolize longevity, and because of the large number of seeds in them, the wish for many sons. Double gourds, as a motif, appear often on snuff bottles made from a variety of materials, including jade, porcelain, and glass among others. Bottles were also produced in the shape of double gourds, with some made from gourds themselves. Additional meanings attributed to the double gourd include the upper bulb symbolizing heaven, or the heavenly place to where one aspires, and the lower bulb the earthly realm, where one lives. The symbolic importance of the double gourd, including at the imperial court, cannot be underestimated. The *Archives of the Imperial Household Department* show that in 1754 the Box Workshop was ordered to make a container to safely hold a double gourd–shaped glass flower holder in opaque-green with blue overlay. The listing specified that the item would be kept at the palace (rather than given as a gift), indicating the treasured status of the vase.

Jadeite

Jadeite (*feitsui*) has been highly prized by the Chinese for centuries. It was known to them from the late Ming dynasty but did not become a treasured material until the last quarter of the Qianlong reign when it became accepted at court as a highly valued alternative form of jade. Likely, the material was first mined in the later years of the eighteenth century. The stone is harder than jade but brittle so difficult to carve. Whilst the purest emerald-green jadeite was infrequently fashioned into snuff bottles, apple-green jadeite was used more often. Such was the fascination for the stone that it rapidly became a material favored by the Qianlong Emperor and his extensive family.

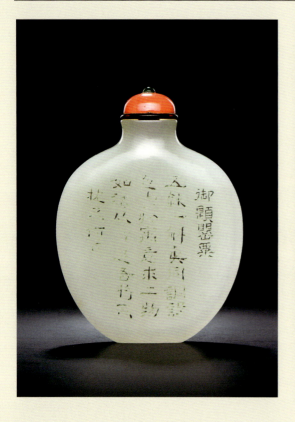

32

清乾隆　白玉御題詩「罌粟金錢」鼻煙壺

鼻煙壺白玉雕成。短頸，溜肩，扁圓腹，腹下漸收，凹底。腹壁兩面陰刻填金花卉詩文，一面刻緩坡草地生數株罌粟花卉，花葉扶疏，朵花嬌豔，一派臨風搖曳的嬌豔模樣。另一面則陰刻字體工整的「御題罌粟」七言詩，詩曰：「五銖一斛真同調，設色當於寓意求。二物如誠比戶足，吾將高枕又何憂。」

考是詩乃乾隆皇帝作於癸未（1763）年〈題錢維城花卉四種〉中的其中一首〈罌粟金錢〉，該詩今收錄於《御製詩三集．卷二十七》。

1736-1795年
高：5.9 厘米

A nephrite bottle, very well hollowed; of flattened rounded form, with rounded shoulders tapering to a cylindrical neck with slightly everted mouth, and tapering at the base to a narrow oval foot; of even white tone; incised on one main side with leafy flowering peonies growing on a grassy bank, the reverse with a calligraphic inscription reading:

"(The flower) truly resembles a small coin lying in a cup,
its meaning found both in that and its color,
if every household held only these things,
I would sleep on a high pillow, with no cares in the world."

beside a *Qianlong yuzhi* mark.

Imperial, attributed to the Palace Workshops, Beijing.

1736-1795
Height: 5.9 cm

一面刻：
「御題罌粟：
五銖一斛真同調，設色當於寓意求。
二物如誠比戶足，吾將高枕又何憂。」

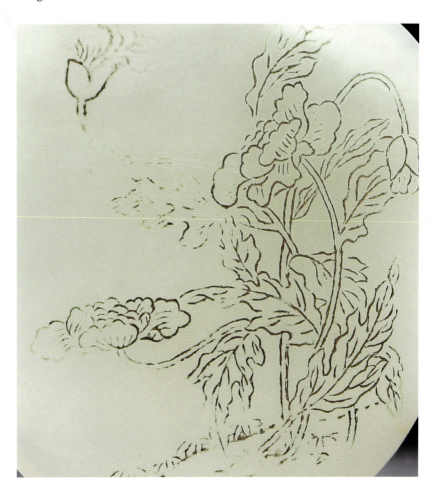

33

清　白玉開光詩文鼻煙壺

鼻煙壺白玉雕成，玉質凝潤潔白。通體作扁瓶形。敞口，束頸，溜肩，扁弧腹，腹部近底足處漸收，凹底。全器兩面雕工，皆以二方連續方雷紋圈圍成圓形開光。開光內一面浮雕篆體詩句「春游芳草地，夏賞綠荷池」，另一面則接續詩句下聯「秋飲黃菊酒，冬吟白雪詩」。所鐫詩句形態肅穆，遒勁圓勻，敦厚雍容，具力透紙背般的筆墨韻致。

考「春遊芳草地」等四句，乃出自北宋汪洙所編寫的〈神童詩〉，該詩甚長，總計五言九十聯，如大家耳熟能詳的「久旱逢甘雨，他鄉遇故知；洞房花燭夜，金榜題名時」即是收錄於該詩的其中二聯。本件鼻煙壺所刻詩句，據悉為該詩的最末二聯。

1736-1795年
高：5.8 厘米

兩面浮雕：

「春游芳草地，夏賞綠荷池，
秋飲黃菊酒，冬吟白雪詩。」

A nephrite bottle, very well hollowed; of flattened rounded form, with rounded shoulders tapering to a cylindrical neck with slightly everted mouth, and tapering at the base to a narrow oval foot; of even white tone; each main side with a central panel carved with a raised calligraphic inscription in archaic script reading on one side:

"Spring outing, let's go to the lush green meadow we're so fond of.
Summer is for viewing the green lotus pond."
The reverse:
"Autumn, let's drink the yellow chrysanthemum wine.
Winter brings forth poetry on the pure white snow."

Imperial, attributed to the Palace Workshops, Beijing.

1736-1795
Height: 5.8 cm

34

清　白玉鑲碧玉蒂茄形鼻煙壺

鼻煙壺白玉雕成，作茄瓜形，通體光素，打磨光滑，肩部另以碧玉雕琢花葉且安鑲為蒂托。全器能巧妙運用綠、白兩玉色的完美搭配，一方面配色對比強烈，另方面造型栩栩如生，誠為清代中期的典型宮廷佳作。

是類作品在清宮舊藏中不乏有組構十件配以木匣珍藏的案例。

1750-1795年
高：7 厘米

A nephrite bottle, very well hollowed; of even white tone carved in the form of a plump eggplant with a detailed spinach-green jade calyx; the stopper carved as its stalk.

Imperial, attributed to the Palace Workshops, Beijing.

1750-1795
Height: 7 cm

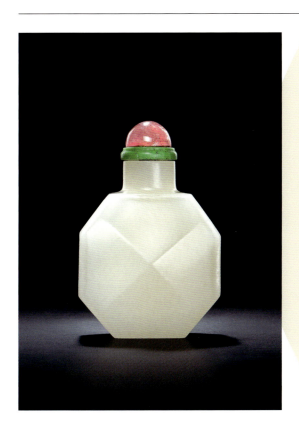

35

清　白玉磨稜八角形鼻煙壺

鼻煙壺白玉雕成，呈扁瓶形。直口，斜削肩，八角形腹，平底。通體一任光素，不施任何具象的裝飾紋樣。腹部兩面磨切成四斜坡幾何形，且至中心點錐凸高起。是類八角形鼻煙壺看似簡單平凡，但從八角造型到斜坡腹壁的起線安排，在在都考驗著創作者的抽象思維是否準確到位，所謂「差以毫釐，失之千里」，欣賞此類作品亦作如是觀。

1750-1795年
高：4.7 厘米

A nephrite bottle, very well hollowed; of even white tone; of octagonal faceted form with raised panels on the front and reverse, carved as diagonally segmented quatrefoils, with a cylindrical neck and a neatly carved flat base.

Imperial, attributed to the Palace Workshops, Beijing.

1750-1795
Height: 4.7 cm

36

清　白玉繩紋獸首貫耳鼻煙壺

白玉鼻煙壺，呈扁瓶形。直口，短束頸，折肩，深腹，腹下漸收，下承高束腰方圈足。腹壁兩面中心淺浮雕一玉璧，玉璧四端刻飾有雙繫繩紋，繩紋自玉璧呈交錯狀向腹壁四周貼繞。肩部兩側浮雕一對獸面耳，兩側壁從獸面底部至圈足處貫以溝槽，可穿繩提掛。全器雕工典雅，設計巧妙，是清代中期的典型宮廷作品。

1750-1795年
高：5.7 厘米

A nephrite bottle, very well hollowed; of even white tone; of tapering, rectangular form, with a cylindrical neck and straightened everted mouth, and standing on a slightly splayed foot, carved on each main side within a border following the edges of the bottle, with a cash symbol tied with four strands of twisted rope, the shoulders carved in relief with mock mask handles, the narrow sides each with a vertical channel for threading a silk cord, with a pierced hole at the footrim.

Imperial, attributed to the Palace Workshops, Beijing.

1750-1795
Height: 5.7 cm

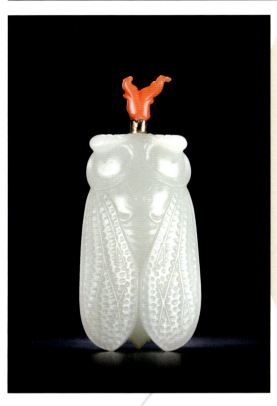

清　白玉蟬形鼻煙壺

鼻煙壺白玉雕成，作象生蟬形，兩面雕工，胎體厚實。複眼突出，頸部飾有數道陰刻弧狀弦紋，增添典雅氣息。雙翅以桯鑽打窪，並以細線紋表現翅脈，營造輕靈的穿透視覺效果。背後蟬足屈曲寫實，腹節層層疊壓，周緣鋸齒狀的勾勒與每層腹節底邊的短平行線點綴，都清楚說明創作者一絲不苟的美學追求，將之歸屬象生鼻煙壺的上乘之作，當無過譽也。

1750-1795年
高：6.8 厘米

A nephrite bottle, very well hollowed; of even white tone; carved in the form of a resting cicada with folded wings.

Imperial, attributed to the Palace Workshops.

1750-1795
Height: 6.8 cm

38

清　白玉菊瓣紋鼻煙壺

鼻煙壺白玉雕成，玉質潔白無瑕，凝潤細膩。通體呈菊瓣形。
直口，短頸，豐肩，腹下漸收，橢圓形圈足。腹壁做規律的菊
瓣紋，菊瓣中間起棱，兩瓣之間的低谷處，復以雙陰刻線表現
一道凸棱。全器造型飽滿，線條流暢，簡潔明快，彌顯珍貴。

1750-1795年
高：5.2 厘米

A nephrite bottle, very well hollowed; of even white tone;
of slightly bulbous shield shape, with a cylindrical neck
with a straightened mouth; the body carved with vertical
undulating panels divided by a ridged edge, tapering to a
scalloped flat base.

Imperial, attributed to the Palace Workshops.

1750-1795
Height: 5.2 cm

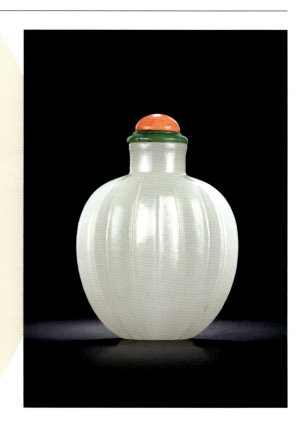

清　白玉雕「繹堂」款獸面紋鼻煙壺

鼻煙壺白玉雕，玉質溫潤。呈長瓶形。直口，溜肩，深腹，腹部飽滿，至底部漸收，橢圓形圈足。腹壁兩面淺浮雕獸面紋，獸面甚巨，約佔腹壁的二分之一，具有舞獅面具的風韻。兩側壁淺浮雕變形雲紋，底陰刻「繹堂」二字篆書款。

考「繹堂」或指乾隆朝進士那彥成（1764-1833年），其字韶九，號繹堂，工書，滿州正白旗人。

1780-1833年
高：6.2 厘米

A nephrite bottle, very well hollowed; of even white tone; of rectangular form, with rounded shoulders sloping to a cylindrical neck, and with a neatly carved oval footrim, carved on each main side with a *taotie* mask; the base with a mark in archaic script reading: *Yitang*.

Imperial, attributed to the Palace Workshops, Beijing.

1780-1833
Height: 6.2 cm

40

清　白玉高浮雕蟠螭紋鼻煙壺

白玉鼻煙壺，呈扁瓶形。敞口，束頸，豐肩，扁深腹，腹下漸收，圈足。腹壁兩面以剔地技法，各飾一尾高浮雕螭龍，螭龍軀體修長，做匍匐爬行貌，一面向上，一面向下，展現前後遙相凝望的嬉戲意趣。

是件鼻煙壺似刻意追求清雅韻致，視覺重點集中蟠螭的刻畫，所刻螭龍具神武英姿，以致也提昇了鼻煙壺的藝術觀賞價值。

1750-1795年
高：6.3 厘米

A nephrite bottle, very well hollowed; of even white tone with a russet inclusion; of *meiping* form, with a cylindrical neck and everted straightened mouth, and with an oval foot; carved in relief on each main side with a coiling *kui* dragon.

Imperial, attributed to the Palace Workshops, Beijing.

1750-1795
Height: 6.3 cm

41

清　白玉雲蝠紋葫蘆形束腰活環鼻煙壺

鼻煙壺和闐子玉雕成，局部有褐色斑。敞口，鼓肩，束腰，圓腹，圜底，通體呈葫蘆形，束腰處鏤飾一活環。全器滿飾淺浮雕雲蝠紋，蝙蝠五隻，盤旋祥雲之間。據此連結活環的圓滿意象與葫蘆的「祿」之音轉，遂有「五福臨門，福祿圓滿」的美好寓意。

1750-1795年
高：6.1 厘米

A nephrite bottle, very well hollowed, of double gourd form resting on a small concave base, with cylindrical neck with an everted straightened mouth, the mid-section of the gourd encircled by a loose ring, the stone of a pale-yellow color with russet-brown inclusions, the upper and lower bulbs carved in low relief with a continuous horizontal band of five bats flying in vapor.

Imperial, attributed to the Palace Workshops, Beijing.

1750-1795
Height: 6.1 cm

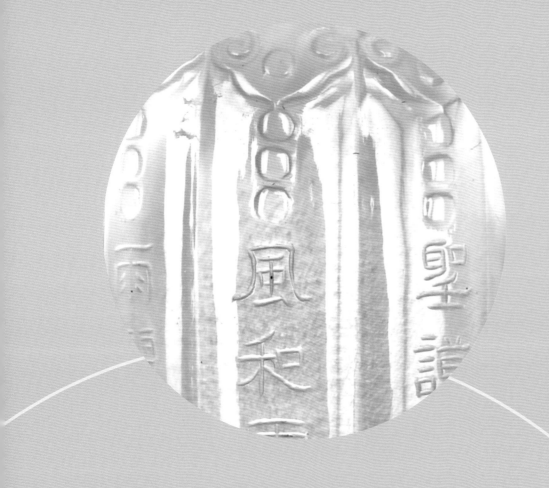

玉髓與瑪瑙

當滿人選址北京，建立清王朝時，為了同化以及取得漢人的信任，他們極力吸取當地漢人的文化。儘管吸食鼻烟是清朝特有的現象，存放鼻烟的器皿則展現了漢人的文化遺韻。康熙皇帝是歷史上有名的藝術贊助人，自1680年始，他在京城宮廷內設立各式作坊，並在京外蘇州等地設玉石作坊。

在宮中，工匠挑選上好的石材製作鼻煙壺與其他文房珍玩。「雲狀瑪瑙」，是一個寶石名詞，指帶有棉絮狀內含物的灰色瑪瑙。部分掏膛工整的冰糖瑪瑙鼻煙壺，其雲狀內含物所呈的圖案深深地吸引了廣大藏家，這種美不是源于精美的加工工藝，而是源于石頭本身的構造 —— 六方柱形晶體結構。

一般而言，宮廷冰糖瑪瑙（雲狀瑪瑙）鼻煙壺的內腔工藝超群，淡灰色，帶棉絮石紋，器形多與玉鼻煙壺相近。有一類鼻煙壺十分著名，柱形，腹部八方開光，上刻與乾隆皇帝相關的詩文，底部一般落「乾隆年製」四字刻款。根據這些御題詩，我們可以明確這類鼻烟壺乃內務府造辦處所製。根據多件同類鼻煙壺可知，雖然這類鼻烟壺顏色的深淺不一，但多呈淺灰色，或因成套訂制，或因清末宮內流行。

宮廷瑪瑙鼻煙壺大多擁有相同特徵，也與造辦處所製玉鼻煙壺有相似之處。典型的宮廷特徵主要有器形小巧以及突出的形式化裝飾風格。仿古紋樣間飾雙龍紋、邊緣飾絞絲紋、頸部飾蕉葉紋常見於造辦處所製玉、瑪瑙以及料胎鼻煙壺。造辦處乃行政機構，監管各個宮廷作坊，構建一個給各個作坊分配任務的系統，制定各式設計與製作各類珍玩。造辦處內監管人員不多，他們身負重任，確保各件器物按旨意製作，不允許工匠在製作過程中加入個人創意，按旨意發揮他們的技藝。如今，我們無法得知這些作品分別是哪位工匠所製，因為大多沒有款識或僅有當朝年款。即使有部分作品在宮外製作，而後被送入宮中，工匠的流動也給內廷帶來了各種新想法，但宮廷樣式往往被迅速強加給各位工匠。

鼻煙壺是一種適合社交藝術形式，用於朋友間的交流、流轉，給觀賞者讚揚其主人的機會，不僅彰顯主人財富，亦體現了主人對生活中高品質珍玩的追求。因此，它迅速成為一個完美的收藏對象。眾所周知，乾隆寵臣和珅有一個龐大的鼻烟壺收藏，約1400件，在他被賜自盡後，被全部沒收，後分賜宮中各處。

乾隆中期始，吸食鼻烟成為了宮中一個社交風尚，簡潔以及簡易的容器已經無法滿足大家的需求，宮廷作坊迅速做出反應，大量生產各種材質的鼻烟壺。

CHALCEDONY

In order to assimilate and gain the trust of the Han people, as the Manchu established themselves in Beijing, and formed the Qing dynasty, they endeavored to acquire the culture of the existing population. And although snuff appears to be exclusively a Qing phenomenon, the containers for snuff exposed the legacy of a more cultured people. The Kangxi Emperor became a great patron of the arts through the setting up of imperial workshops both within the confines of the palace in Beijing after 1680, and in areas such as Suzhou for jades and hardstones.

Within the palace, the best stones were used in the carving of snuff bottles and other scholar's objects. The term 'cloud agate' is one used by gemologists and is defined as a grayish agate with blurry foggy patches of inclusions. The cloud-like patterns in very well-hollowed chalcedony examples, which are so attractive to collectors, are not formed by clever internal polishing of the bottle but are part of the composition of the stone – the visible six-sided prisms of the crystalline structure.

Imperial bottles fashioned from chalcedony, or 'cloud agate', are generally superbly hollowed, of dappled pale gray tones, and often in forms that follow jade bottles. One well-known group is of tapering cylindrical form, carved with eight vertical lobed panels incised with a poem directly connecting the bottle to the Qianlong Emperor, and often with the base inscribed in seal script *Qianlong nian zhi* (made in the Qianlong period). With such illustrious inscriptions, this group can be attributed to the Palace Workshops. There are several bottles from this group published, and it seems that they were made in a variety of shades of agate, though most of them seem to be in similar tones of pale gray suggesting that these bottles were either made in sets or were simply very popular in the late Qianlong court.

Often imperial agate bottles share common features that they also share with jade bottles from the Palace Workshops. Typical 'palace' features include - the shape, the small size, and primarily its formal decorative features. Confronting dragons between archaic borders, rope twist edges, and neck borders of Artemis leaves appear on jade, agate, and glass bottles that can be attributed to the Palace Workshops. The *Zaobanchu,* the administrative office, which controlled the Palace Workshops, provided a system that dictated to the workshops pre-ordained designs and orders for the pieces. The influential minority who had the responsibility passed to them for ordering the pieces would have had little tolerance of the creativity of the craftsmen, merely utilizing their exceptional skills to produce what was required. The output in this sense is anonymous, as the piece might not have a mark on it or simply the reign mark of the ruling emperor. Even given the facts that some pieces were made elsewhere and sent up to the palace, and allowing for the cross-fertilization of ideas due to the movement of workers, a palace-style would have quickly been imposed upon craftsmen.

The snuff bottle was a very social art form. It was designed to be brought out amongst friends, and handed around, giving the recipients a chance to compliment its owner and enabling him to demonstrate not only his wealth but also his appreciation of the finer things in life. As such it quickly became the perfect collector's item. It is well known that He Shen, Qianlong's chief minister had a prolific collection of bottles, around 1400, which were confiscated and redistributed in the court after his forced suicide.

It appears then, that by the mid-Qianlong period taking snuff had acquired a social cachet in the court, which required more than a plain disposable container, and the imperial workshops quickly began to fulfill that need using bottles fashioned from a wide variety of materials.

42

清乾隆　菊瓣形冰糖瑪瑙題「平定兩金川」鼻煙壺

鼻煙壺冰糖瑪瑙雕成，半透明質地。作長罐形，圈足。頸部飾一圈團花，肩部淺浮雕如意雲肩垂珠紋一匝，腹壁鏤刻成菊瓣式，每瓣並填刻詩文，依序是：「殊域宣威奏蕩平，聖謨遠屆武功成。風和雪嶺春消燧，雨灑桃關夜洗兵。通道昔年淶貢馬，受俘今日獲長鯨。從今坤徼都無險，萬里提封接塞城。」又，近底足處淺浮雕變形蓮瓣紋一圈，底部鎸「乾隆年製」兩行四字篆書款。

考〈殊域宣威奏蕩平〉七言律詩，為乾隆朝大學士阿桂所撰〈平定兩金川〉十二首組詩裡的其中一首。

1750-1795年
高：6.5 厘米

A chalcedony bottle, superbly hollowed; of dappled pale gray tones; of tapering cylindrical form with shoulders sloping to an everted mouth, and with a neatly carved footrim; the main body with eight vertical lobes rising from a band of formalized lotus petals around the base and ending at the shoulders in a mantel of formalized *lingzhi* heads, each set above three raised bosses to simulate pendant jewels, the neck with a single band of two alternating flowerheads; the lobed panels incised with an imperial poem reading:

"His Majesty's rule reaches to distant lands, showing great success in military achievements,
the gentle wind blows on the Snow Mountains where fires were lit in the spring evenings,
night rain showers the Gateway of Taoguan, washes the army clean at the passageway,
where tribute horses passed through last year. Today at the ceremony where our chief enemy
surrenders and is captured, we know that every border of our land will be free from danger,
our territory of a thousand miles is strengthened by this frontier city, our might is shown here,
and in faraway lands."

the base inscribed in seal script *Qianlong nian zhi,* and of the period.

Imperial, attributed to the Palace Workshops, Beijing.

1750-1795
Height: 6.5 cm

詩文：
「殊域宣威奏蕩平，聖謨遠居武功成。
風和雪嶺春宵燧，雨灑桃關夜洗兵。
通道昔年淶貢馬，受俘今日獲長鯨。
從今坤徼都無險，萬里提封接塞城。」

底鎸兩行四字款：
「乾隆年製」

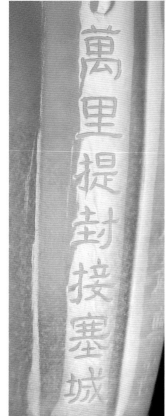

43

清　冰糖瑪瑙雕勾連雲紋鼻煙壺

鼻煙壺冰糖瑪瑙雕成，半透明質地。呈罐形。直口，深腹，平底。通體腹壁滿飾淺浮雕四方連續的變形勾連雲紋，勾連雲紋上下四方延展自有秩序，惟重複的意象，自然也營造出宛如萬花筒般的繽紛視覺律動，是一件雕工精美且具有典雅風尚的玲瓏珍玩。

1750-1795年
高：5.8 厘米

A chalcedony bottle, superbly hollowed; of dappled pale gray tones; of tapering cylindrical form with shoulders sloping to an everted mouth, and with a neatly carved foot; the main body continuously carved with bands of comma scrolls and raised bosses.

Imperial, attributed to the Palace Workshops, Beijing.

1750-1795
Height: 5.8 cm

44

清　冰糖瑪瑙開光詩紋鼻煙壺

冰糖瑪瑙腦鼻煙壺，通體作扁瓶形。敞口，束頸，溜肩，扁弧腹，腹部至底足處漸收，凹底。全器兩面雕工，皆以二方連續方雷紋圈圍成圓形開光。開光內一面浮雕篆體詩句「春游芳草地，夏賞綠荷池」，另一面則接續詩句下聯「秋飲黃菊酒，冬吟白雪詩」。

本件作品與編號33基本相同，相關補充説明可參見33號作品。

1736-1795年
高：6.1 厘米

A chalcedony bottle, very well hollowed; of flattened rounded form, with rounded shoulders tapering to a cylindrical neck with slightly everted mouth, and tapering at the base to a narrow oval foot; of dappled pale-grey tone; each main side with a central panel carved with a raised calligraphic inscription in archaic script reading on one side:

"Spring outing, let's go to the lush green meadow we're so fond of.
Summer is for viewing the green lotus pond."
The reverse:
"Autumn, let's drink the yellow chrysanthemum wine.
Winter brings forth poetry on the pure white snow."

Imperial, attributed to the Palace Workshops, Beijing.

1736-1795
Height: 6.1 cm

兩面浮雕：
「春游芳草地，
夏賞綠荷池，
秋飲黃菊酒，
冬吟白雪詩。」

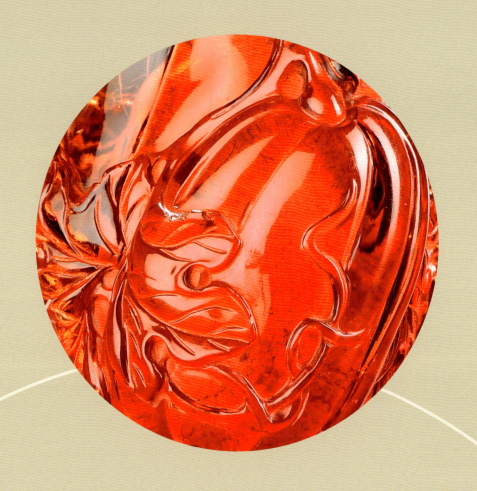

宮廷有機材料鼻煙壺

剔紅

漆雕是一種十二世紀創於中國的雕刻漆器。此工藝,先層層髹塗紅漆,再於其上進行雕刻,十分耗時,因此,被視為奢華之物。在清代,此工藝常用於裝飾小件器物,如盤、盒、鼻煙壺等,多在木胎上髹漆,同時,也有一些尺寸稍大的器物,如盆、箱櫃,以及更稀有的傢俱作品,如桌子。製作此工藝的過程被稱為雕漆。明以前,漆器雕刻多飾剔犀雲紋,日本稱屈輪 (guri),隨後,剔紅,這種帶浮雕紋飾的紅色漆器開始流行,常見剔紅雕山水人物圖、五爪龍紋以及花鳥紋。

明早期,宮廷漆器作坊稱果園廠,1416年設於紫禁城旁靈境胡同一帶。來自南方浙江嘉興、雲南以及四川的工匠們被選派至此。近5000名工匠從南方被招進宮廷各個作坊任職,任期不超過四年。因為北京無法種植漆樹,祇能從南方運來新鮮的漆液。果園廠前後運作了二十年,隨著漆器生產的減少,於1436年關閉。

到了十七世紀末，1680年，康熙皇帝設立多個宮廷作坊，其中便有漆器作坊。因乾隆皇帝喜愛雕漆，漆作在十八世紀十分活躍。1799年，乾隆皇帝駕崩，其後宮廷生產的雕漆無論是數量上還是質量上均大不如前。十八世紀的鼻煙壺大多風格統一，通過高浮雕的工藝於盾牌形狀的木胎上雕飾山水人物圖。

琥珀

琥珀是一種樹脂化石，形成於成岩作用，而不是大家所認為的樹的汁液。自新石器時代，琥珀便以其自然的魅力、顏色以及其趨吉避凶的能量吸引大家。它源自軟而黏稠的樹脂，常帶植物或動物等內含物。

歷史上，最早記載琥珀的文獻可追溯到西元前4世紀，希臘哲學家提奧夫拉斯圖斯所著。英文amber一詞自十五世紀初開始被使用，它源於阿拉伯文anbar、中世紀拉丁文ambar以及古法文ambre。

琥珀輕於石頭，但在固體狀態下又無法浮於水面。源自俄羅斯的波羅的海琥珀或被海浪沖上岸或被直接挖掘開採，自古代起便被頻繁交易。鼻煙壺藏家們認為不透明的黃色和褐色的琥珀是波羅的海琥珀，但不是所有產自波羅的海的琥珀均不透明。

在中國，有一種不透明黃色或紅色的物質叫蜜蠟，容易與波羅的海琥珀相混淆，歷史上它被冠以了很多不同的稱謂，如琥珀、蜜蠟、遺玉等。稱呼隨著時間和區域有所不同。如今，我們知道蜜蠟和琥珀是兩種不同的物質。蜜蠟形成於兩千萬至一億年前，而波羅的海琥珀則形成於四百至五百萬年前。

琥珀鼻煙壺的顏色多樣，有檸檬黃、橙、褐、紅以及黑色。部分十八世紀生產的宮廷琥珀鼻煙壺的器形、雕刻風格與同時期宮廷作坊生產的玉鼻煙壺相似。

ORGANIC

Cinnabar Lacquer

Carved lacquer or *Qidiao* is a type of carved lacquerware that was developed in China in the 12th century. The technique of carving into layered coatings of lacquer is very time-consuming and as such lacquerware was considered to be a luxury item. It was mostly used to fashion small objects such as dishes, boxes, and snuff bottles in the Qing dynasty, generally with the layers of lacquer on a wood base, although there are examples of larger chargers and cabinets, and more rarely, pieces of furniture, such as tables. The production process is called *Diaoqi*, or 'carving lacquer.' Before the early Ming period lacquer carving followed the abstract *guri*, or 'sword-pommel' pattern, but subsequently, the relief carved red lacquer known as cinnabar lacquer became more popular with vessels and containers being carved with figures in a mountainous landscape, imperial dragons, and birds and flowers.

In the early Ming period, the imperial workshop known as the 'Orchard Workshop' was founded, around 1416 in Lingjing Hutong near the Forbidden City. Workers from the south were sent there from Jiaxing in Zhejiang province, and also from Yunnan and Sichuan. Approximately 5,000 workers from the south were employed to work in the imperial workshops for up to four years at a time. Raw lacquer was also imported from the south as the Chinese lacquer tree did not grow as far north as Beijing. After twenty years the Orchard Workshop closed in 1436 when the production of lacquerwares diminished.

At the end of the 17th century, the imperial workshops were founded by the Kangxi Emperor in 1680, of which one was a lacquer workshop. This continued throughout the 18th century as the Qianlong Emperor was extremely fond of carved lacquer. After his death in 1799, imperial production of carved lacquer experienced a steep decline in terms of both quality and quantity of pieces. The majority of eighteenth-century snuff bottles seem to follow a similar style and subject matter generally of figures in a mountainous landscape carved in high relief on a shield-shaped wood body.

Amber

Amber is a fossilized tree resin and not, as some collectors think, sap, and occurs in rock formations. It has been appreciated since Neolithic times for its natural organic beauty, color, and healing powers. It originates as a soft sticky tree resin sometimes containing plant and animal inclusions.

The first historical mention of the material amber was possibly by the Greek philosopher, Theophrastus in the 4th century BCE. The English term 'amber' has been used since the beginning of the 15th century and is derived from the Arabic word 'anbar' via Medieval Latin ('ambar') and Old French ('ambre').

Amber is lighter than stone but in its solid form not light enough to float in water. Amber from the Baltic Sea in Russia is either cast up by the waves or mined and has been extensively traded since antiquity. Snuff bottle collectors refer to opaque yellow or brown amber as Baltic amber, but not all amber that comes from that region is opaque.

In China, there is also a type of opaque yellow or red material called beeswax, often confused with Baltic amber, which has over the years been given several names, such as Hupo, Mila, Yiyu, and so on. The names vary according to the region and historically. It is known today that beeswax and amber are different minerals. Beeswax was formed between 20 million to 100 million years ago, while Baltic amber was formed four to five million years ago.

Amber snuff bottles come in a range of colors from lemon yellow, through orange to brown and even red and black. Many of the shapes and styles of carving of imperially attributed amber bottles lie in parallel with jade snuff bottles produced in the imperial workshops in the 18th century.

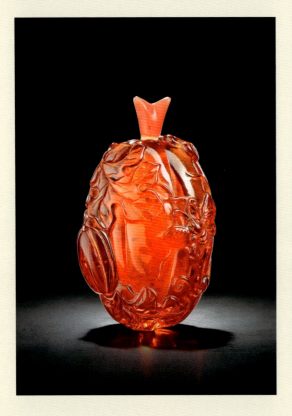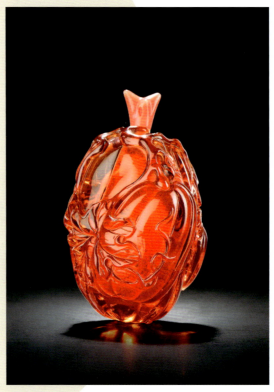

45

清　琥珀「瓜瓞綿綿」鼻煙壺

鼻煙壺整料琥珀雕成，半透明深紅色，作瓜形。腹體碩實飽
滿，外壁淺浮雕蔓葉翻捲，此間大葉開張緊貼腹壁，絲絲蔓藤
纏繞左右，蔓藤上並有小瓜垂掛，而蝴蝶翩翩飛舞一隅，能用
精美的圖畫意象，形塑表徵子孫萬代的瓜瓞綿綿吉祥寓意，誠
然令人激賞。

1750-1795年
高：5 厘米

An amber bottle, very well hollowed; of clear, rich honey-brown tones; carved in the form of a ripe gourd with smaller gourds and a butterfly carved in relief among twisting leafy flowering vines.

Imperial, attributed to the Palace Workshops, Beijing.

1750-1795
Height: 5 cm

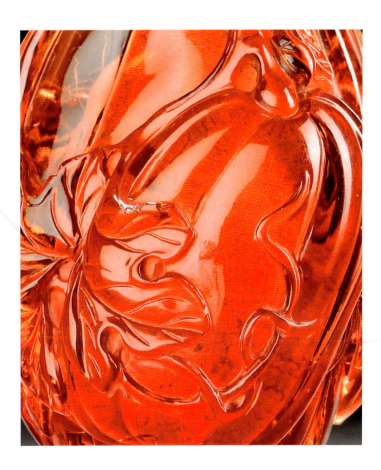

46

清　剔紅纏枝牡丹紋鼻煙壺

鼻煙壺金屬胎。敞口，短頸，豐肩，扁圓腹，腹下急斂，圈足。通體髹堆厚朱漆，然後以剔紅技法，於頸部飾二方連續卍字錦地寬帶紋一圈，近底足處則雕飾一匝做上下相對的連續方折幾何紋，腹部的主題紋樣滿飾表徵萬代富貴的菊紋錦地纏枝牡丹紋。

是件剔紅鼻煙壺，漆色鮮豔，雕工纖細，刻劃鮮活，具有清中期的典型雕漆特徵。

1750-1795年
高：5.7 厘米

A cinnabar lacquer on wood bottle, of shield shape with rounded shoulders tapering to a flared cylindrical neck, and at the base with a flat oval foot; continuously carved in relief with flowering peonies amongst scrolling leafy vines reserved against a diaper ground, between a band of *lingzhi* heads around the shoulders and a *leiwen* band around the foot, the neck with a Buddhist swastika pattern, the mouth with a gilded bronze collar; with original matching stopper.

Imperial, attributed to the Palace Workshops, Beijing.

1750-1795
Height: 5.7 cm

47

清 匏制開光「玉堂蘭石」鼻煙壺

鼻煙壺以葫蘆套範成形，腹壁、側面與底足猶可見合模線痕。壺作扁瓶形。直口，豐肩，腹部厚實飽滿，腹下漸收，平底。兩肩處飾一對獸首銜環，腹壁兩面皆開光，開光內飾淺浮雕洞石海棠玉蘭花卉，也即是文人畫常見的「玉堂蘭石」圖題材。是圖線條明快爽朗，頗具白描勾勒的筆墨韻致。

1750-1800年
高：5.5 厘米

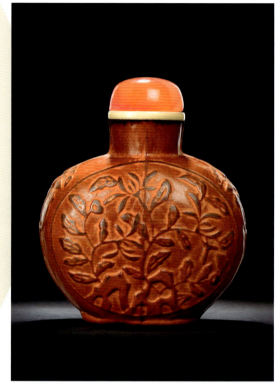

A gourd bottle, well patinated, of bulbous rounded form, with a cylindrical neck and a flat oval foot; molded with a design within a circular panel of leafy flowers issuing from convoluted rockwork, the narrow sides with mock mask and ring handles; the material of a rich golden-brown color.

Imperial, attributed to the Palace Workshops, Beijing.

1750-1800
Height: 5.5 cm

其他工作坊與流派
OTHER WORKSHOPS and SCHOOLS

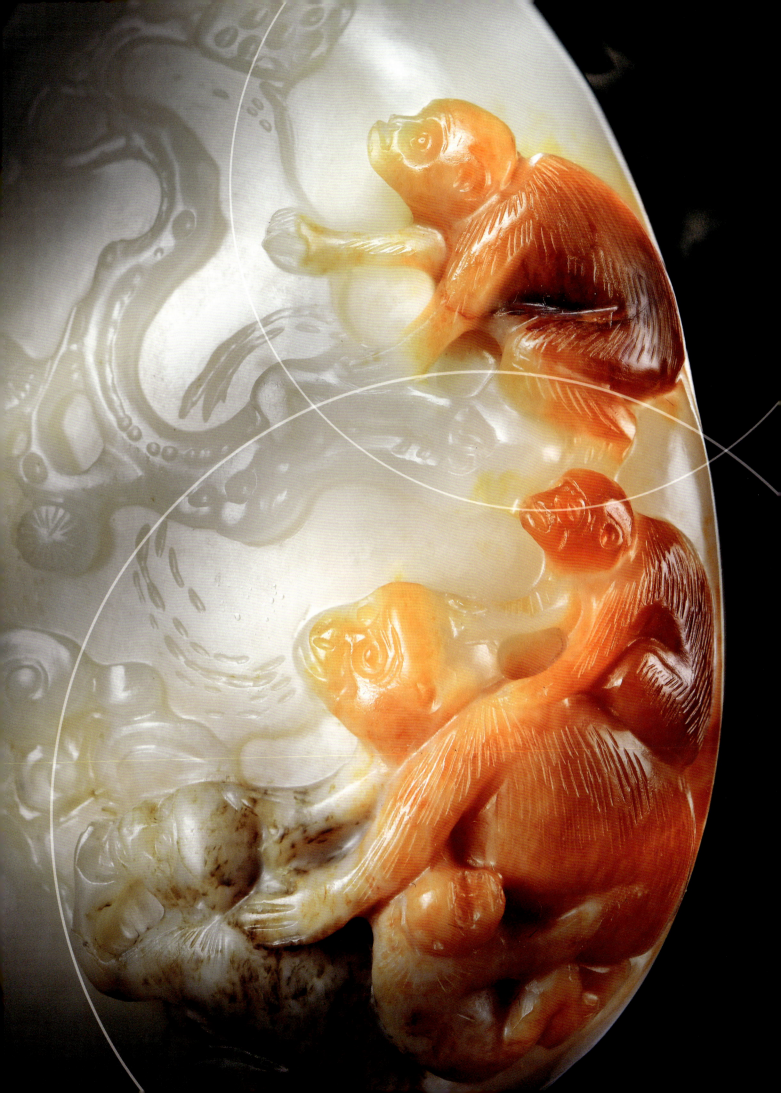

景德鎮

早在唐代（618-907年），景德鎮便開始生產瓷器，作為貢品被送往宮廷，這顯示了當時生產工藝之高。到了宋代（960-1279年），景德鎮以瓷器生產聞名，當時共有約300個生產瓷器的窯口。元代（1271-1368年），青花瓷器的出現鞏固了景德鎮作為中國瓷都的地位。

明代（1368-1644年）首設御窯廠，由於景德鎮山區的高嶺土含量豐富，御窯廠的設立並未阻礙當地其他窯口的繁榮發展。高嶺土是瓷器胎土中最重要的成份。景德鎮四周被森林包圍，為瓷器的燒造提供了充足的燃料。瓷業在景德鎮興盛的同時，參與瓷器各個生產環節的人口也逐漸增加，常見整個家族均參與與瓷器生產相關的行業。當地有販賣胎土的商鋪、燒窯所用木材的商鋪、素胎商鋪、松木商鋪、繪製瓷器的商鋪、打包舖（用禾稈）、匣缽廠（燒瓷時用於裝載瓷器的器皿）、瓷器貿易公司，還有各式商店。其他商鋪和作坊均從事與瓷器燒造相關的周邊行業，如陶製量器、模具修復、瓷胎切割、筆具、顏料，以及把瓷器運往全國各地或通過海上絲綢之路運往西方的船運公司。

清代（1644-1911年）瓷器生產更多種多樣，出現各式新風格，質量高低不同。有的為宮廷特製，有的為國內市場所製，也有的為出口海外所製。大量的家庭作坊為國內貴族階級生產高品質的瓷器，它們可以生產一些非宮廷作坊製作，但質量可與宮廷作坊媲美的瓷器。其他窯口則服務於本地市場與海外市場。

自嘉慶起（1796-1820年），除御窯廠外，景德鎮其他窯坊亦生產了大量瓷胎鼻煙壺，是瓷器流行與鼻煙壺渴求的結果。這是一個鞏固與創新的時期。在這之前，瓷胎鼻煙壺大多產於景德鎮御窯廠。當吸食鼻煙逐漸普及，宮外對鼻煙壺的需求逐漸增加，工匠們開始生產一些新式、器形新穎的鼻煙壺。這些新奇的器形包括側臥仕女、劉海立像、動物如贔屓、仿生類如蓮蓬。十九世紀生產了大量繪有三國和西遊記等文學故事畫片的瓷胎鼻煙壺。

1855年，正直太平天國時期，太平軍銷毀了景德鎮全部約9000個窯口。叛亂平息後，窯口得以重建，並在1866年後逐步恢復生產。其中包括了御窯廠，它屬於最早被重建的窯口之一。因此1866-1874年間帶「同治年製」款的同治本朝鼻煙壺十分稀有。

十九世紀下半葉，景德鎮各窯口逐漸振興，興起了復古時尚，同時流行落寄託款，如「成化年製」款、「雍正年製」款。光緒時（1875-1908年），景德鎮瓷器生產繁榮，受益於慈禧太后對瓷器的喜愛，根據前朝風格，仿製了一批精美的瓷胎彩繪鼻煙壺。當時，為吸食鼻煙的百姓生產了很多標準化的模製鼻煙壺。這類瓷胎鼻煙壺製作的成功取決於模具是否堅硬，雕工是否精美，胎表面所施釉面是否瑩潤光滑。

素胎瓷器

十九世紀上半葉，在景德鎮有一批工匠製作了一些十分特別的素胎無釉的鼻煙壺以及文房珍玩，有素胎無釉，也有罩施一層淡淡的淺黃釉、芥末黃釉、或檸檬綠釉。

王炳榮、陳國治、李裕成是這個類別公認的大師，擅長製作鼻煙壺等文人珍玩。在一重要文獻裡，稱陳國治為藝人、李裕成為藝術家、王炳榮為商人，此形容十分恰當。這並不意味著王炳榮的作品不受歡迎，而是他的產量相當高。他不僅設計了「松鶴延年」畫片，亦精通人物題材，創作了很多延續傳統風格且細節精美的作品。

我們一般認為，王炳榮擅長精緻的小品，而陳國治則擅長大器。在技術上，無論是減地還是浮雕，鏤雕還是堆塑，人物還是風景，王炳榮均擅長。多樣化的同時，他延續了傳統風格，仿竹雕，甚至把竹雕表面光滑以及乾淨俐落的感覺都能充分表現出來。有趣的是，他稍大尺寸的文房作品均有施釉，但他特意用素胎去展示鼻煙壺上更加精細的雕工。

他的作品均無紀年，但通過與陳國治以及其他陶藝家的作品進行比對，我們可以推測他的作品大約創作於1820-1860年間。鼻煙壺雖然小巧，卻展示了他最精湛的技藝，除此之外，他也創作了筆筒以及成套的文房用具包括筆架、花瓶、香爐、小瓶等。現存約有三分之一的素胎鼻煙壺是帶「王炳榮」款或可明確斷定是他或其工作室所製。

JINGDEZHEN

As early as the Tang dynasty (618-907) porcelain was being produced in Jingdezhen and pieces were sent up to the court as imperial tributes, an indication of the quality of production. By the Song dynasty (1126-1260) Jingdezhen was well-known for its porcelain manufacture with as many as 300 kilns already producing wares. The appearance of blue and white porcelain in the Yuan dynasty (1260-1368) solidified the status of Jingdezhen as the porcelain capital of China.

In the Ming dynasty (1368-1644) the first imperial kilns were built, but other kilns also continued to flourish in this area due to the rich supply of kaolin in the hills around Jingdezhen, the clay which was the primary ingredient in the porcelain recipe. Jingdezhen was also surrounded by forests which supplied an ample amount of firewood for the kilns. As the porcelain industry in Jingdezhen flourished, so did the population there who were involved in different ways with the manufacture of porcelain, often with whole families working together. There were white-clay shops, kiln-use firewood shops, porcelain body companies, pine-firewood kilns, porcelain painting shops, packaging shops (using rice straw), xiabo (a box protecting porcelain during firing) factories, porcelain trading companies, and stores. There were also stores and workshops which supported the porcelain industry, such as ceramic jigger shops, mold repairing workshops, ceramic body cuts, brush shops, pigment shops, and shipping companies for the export of porcelain wares to other areas of the country, to other countries along the Silk Road, and across the seas to the west.

The Qing dynasty (1644-1912) brought more varied production, with new styles but also different levels of quality. Porcelain was produced for the imperial court, the domestic market, and for export overseas. There were dozens of family-owned private kilns making very high-quality wares for the Chinese nobility, which were producing porcelain that, whilst not imperial, could at times rival the imperial porcelain that was being produced. Other kilns supplied porcelain to the Chinese domestic and export markets.

The Jiaqing period (1796-1820) onwards saw a huge increase in the quantities of porcelain bottles produced at Jingdezhen outside the imperial kiln complex. This was a result of the popularity of both porcelain as a medium and snuff bottles as a desirable object. It was both a time of consolidation and innovation. During the preceding years, porcelain snuff bottles had been produced predominately at the imperial kilns at Jingdezhen. As the habit of snuff taking became fashionable, the demand from outside the Palace increased and the potters began to produce new and exciting forms in snuff bottles. These novel shapes included figures such as reclining ladies, Liu hai standing figures, animals such as *bixi*, and natural shapes such as curled lotus pods. A large number of porcelain bottles in the 19th century depicted scenes from popular classics such as the *Romance of the Three Kingdoms* or the *Monkey King*.

In 1855 during the Taiping Rebellion, the Taiping forces destroyed all 9,000 kilns in Jingdezhen. After the war was over, the kilns were rebuilt and slowly reopened from 1866 onwards. This included the imperial kilns which were among the first kilns to be reconstructed. Snuff bottles with a *Tongzhi nian zhi* mark, which are of the period, date from after 1866 to 1874, and as such are very rare.

With the revitalization of the kilns at Jingdezhen in the latter part of the nineteenth century, came continued respect for traditional forms together with the use of apocryphal marks such as *Chenghua nian zhi* and *Yongzheng nian zhi*. During the Guangxu period (1874-1908), the porcelain industry at Jingdezhen flourished, aided by the interest in porcelain of Cixi, the Empress Dowager, and some of the finest enameled porcelain was produced in the style of earlier wares. At this time many bottles were produced from standard molds for the snuff-taking public. Success in the production of porcelain bottles depended on how crisp the molding was, how fine the detailed carving was, and how translucent and smooth the glaze lay over the body of the bottle.

Unglazed Porcelain Wares

In Jingdezhen, during the first half of the 19th century, there were a group of potters who made snuff bottles and other scholar's works of art that were distinct in that the majority of them were either left unglazed, in the 'biscuit,' or with a light clear glaze on them in specific tones such as pale yellow, mustard yellow, and lime green.

Wang Bingrong, Chen Guozhi, and Li Yucheng are generally considered to the three masters of this genre in objects catering to the literati which included snuff bottles. While Chen Guozhi has been described in a seminal publication as the 'showman', Li Yucheng as the 'artist', it was Wang who was described rather aptly as the 'businessman.' This is not to say that his work was not consistently good, but that his output was certainly prolific. In the area of figural work, Wang is seen at his finest, producing pieces that are traditional in style and highly detailed.

It appeared that the smaller the item the more competent Wang was, whilst the reverse might be said for Chen Guozhi. In terms of technique, Wang's work ranges from shallow to relief carving, from pierced work to piled work, from figural studies to landscapes. While versatile, his style is traditional and akin to the bamboo carvers of the day even down to leaving the ground smooth and clean. Interestingly, most of his bigger pieces such as scholar's objects are glazed, but he often left his snuff bottles unglazed to show the finer details in his carving.

His pieces are undated but by comparison with Chen Guozhi and other potters, it can be surmised that his working period must have been around 1820-1860. In addition to snuff bottles, where his work seemed to be at its finest in miniature, his studio produced individual items, such as brush pots, and sets – a series of desk objects which included brush rests, spill vases, incense burners, small vases, and so on. Almost a third of the extant bottles in unglazed porcelain are either signed by Wang Bingrong or clearly attributable to him or his studio.

48

清　王炳榮款淡黃釉雕山水亭閣鼻煙壺

鼻煙壺瓷胎，呈扁瓶形。直口，溜肩，深腹，腹下漸收，
橢圓形圈足。腹壁兩面於瓷胎將乾未乾之際，以刀代筆，
鑴通景式的淺浮雕山水亭閣，然後復於表面施罩淡黃色
釉，再入窯燒製而成。所雕山水亭閣，刻劃細膩，宛如工
筆小品。底署「王炳榮作」四字橫書篆體款。

王炳榮乃清代晚期景德鎮雕瓷名家，擅長山水人物題材，
兩岸故宮今猶存有他的相關作品可資參考。

1820-1860年
高：7.6 厘米

A porcelain bottle, of flattened pear-shape with
a long cylindrical neck and an oval footrim;
covered overall in a pale lemon-yellow glaze; the
body molded, applied and carved in relief with a
continuous scene of a figure traversing a bridge in
front of a pavilion set into a mountainous landscape
of leafy trees and massive rockwork; the base with a
raised potter's mark, *Wang Bingrong zuo*.

Attributed to Jingdezhen.

1820-1860
Height: 7.6 cm

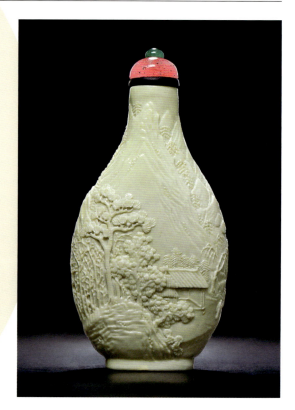

49

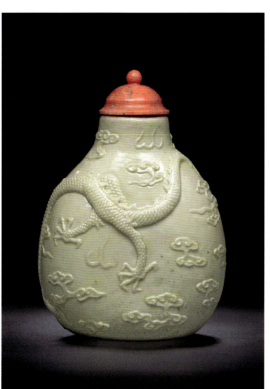

清嘉慶　淡黃釉雕雲龍趕珠紋鼻煙壺

鼻煙壺瓷胎，呈扁瓶形。直口，溜肩，垂腹，腹下漸收，橢圓形臥足。全器裝飾技法與前述雷同，兩腹壁飾淺浮雕雲龍趕珠。是龍引頸低首，張口露齒，身軀屈曲，轉折有力，四周襯以如意祥雲，意味蒼龍飄騰於雲際追趕火雲寶珠，完美展現威猛不可侵犯的皇家氣息。底部署「大清嘉慶年製」三行六字篆書款。

1796-1820年
高：6.2 厘米

A porcelain bottle, of bulbous ovoid form with shoulders sloping to a cylindrical neck and with a concave oval foot; covered overall in a pale lemon-yellow glaze, the body molded, applied and carved in relief with a continuous scene of a coiling scaly dragon flying through scrolling clouds in pursuit of a flaming pearl; the base with a raised six-character mark *Da Qing Jiaqing nianzhi*, and possibly of the period.

Attributed to Jingdezhen.

1796-1820
Height: 6.2 cm

揚州

料器

十八世紀，經濟繁榮，揚州等城市十分富裕。十九世紀，富商們集中在京杭大運河沿線蘇州、揚州等地。該地域的富商們對文化有著新的追求，需要當地的工匠提供一個讓他們可以去模仿他們所仰慕的文人與貴族階層的機會。因此，藝術逐漸發展成一種商業活動。我們可以在繪畫、瓷器以及料器生產上找到很多例證。流傳下來數量眾多的玻璃鼻煙壺，但僅有個別的可以被明確定代為十九世紀。當時的工匠水平良莠不齊，所生產的作品雖然量大，但品質參差不齊。

十八世紀末至十九世紀中葉，料器製作除宮廷以外，全國各地如博山、蘇州和揚州等地亦流行開來。後於十九世紀下半葉在揚州復興。揚州流派所製套料鼻煙壺中有一批數量龐大、特徵鮮明的作品，多作乳白色地，上飾薄薄的單色或多色套料。這批鼻煙壺中約有三分之一刻有詩文、印章或者亭台樓閣的名字。質量參差不齊，雕工有的粗糙劣質，有的精美絕倫。作為商業化的產品，這也是可以理解的，如今我們欣賞這些鼻煙壺既要看其工藝好壞，亦要看其藝術價值。

近年，Hugh Moss 先生和 Stuart Sargent 先生根據新發現的一個刻在鼻煙壺上的人名—李均亭，對揚州流派鼻煙壺進行了重新斷代。李均亭，曾被誤作鼻煙壺工匠，實為十九世紀下半葉居住在揚州的鼻煙壺藏家。約有百分之十的揚州鼻煙壺上刻有紀年款，有時是獨立出現，有時伴隨工匠的款識或詩文。李均亭，活躍於十九世紀晚期，鎮江人，又名維之。這是我們通過多個鼻煙壺上所刻名字與年代的組合所得知，如「靖江李氏」、「均亭」、「維之」或「李」。靖江是鎮江的古名，與揚州相隔八公里，隔江相望。

南方所製的料胎鼻煙壺與銅胎畫琺瑯鼻煙壺多描繪自然景色，反映了當地的自然環境。造型上，揚州與北京套料鼻煙壺相差甚遠。三色套料漁家樂鼻煙壺以及單色套料仙鶴蝙蝠紋鼻煙壺均不如京作鼻煙壺規整。可以明確的是，雖然它們製作時間為十九世紀下半葉，生產地點遠離晚清京城，但其質量與設計仍保持著較高水平。

料胎畫琺瑯

除了宮廷作坊的製品，還有大量料胎畫琺瑯鼻煙壺擁有極高的藝術價值。道光年間，坊間突然出現了一批仿圓明園所製宮廷「古月軒」鼻煙壺，其中不乏精品。這看起來符合邏輯，自1799年乾隆駕崩，此後無需再為其退位後的居所—「古月軒」製作器物。

道光年間，與宮外經濟和政治的困境相比較，宮內陳設的重要性已經變得微不足道了。據了解，道光皇帝曾出讓一些特權，如使用象徵皇家特權黃色的權力。因此，可能缺乏潛在懲罰，「古月軒」款被宮外（北京和揚州）的琺瑯匠人所借用。

除了宮廷作坊，製作琺瑯工藝的中心在哪裡呢？在什麼時代運營的呢？據我們所知，除了京城內的私人作坊，還有揚州、廣州和雲南等琺瑯工藝中心。《揚州畫舫錄》記載了十八世紀雍正、乾隆年間的琺瑯工匠王世雄：「若王世雄，工琺瑯器，好交遊，廣聲氣，京師稱之為『琺瑯王』，又良工也。」

這裡包含了很多信息。王世雄交遊廣（或是客人多），證明了他早在十八世紀上半葉已經營著一個利潤可觀的商業帝國。這反過來也說明了包括鼻煙壺等琺瑯器物已經於宮外廣泛流行。從王世雄的外號「琺瑯王」可知，京城的客人一定有渠道看到他的作品，並可通過京城的商鋪購入。這顯示了當時在京城，假如一名富裕的藏家想要獲取一件精品，可以找遠在揚州的王世雄訂製。

怎樣斷定什麼樣的畫琺瑯鼻煙壺屬於揚州流派風格呢？宮廷外所製鼻煙壺特徵鮮明。雖然某些細節部分，如頸部紋飾、邊飾，仍沿用宮廷制式，但其主體設計常用優雅的自然元素。畫琺瑯鼻煙壺常飾正反面畫片，個別鋪首設計與套料鼻煙壺相近。因商業作坊為了節省成本，琺瑯較薄，不做堆砌。底部款識，多為「古月軒」篆書款，有別於宮廷畫琺瑯鼻煙壺上的「古玉軒」楷書款；或為「乾隆年製」單行篆書款，而非方框款。

YANGZHOU

Glass

During the 18th century cities such as Yangzhou were extraordinarily wealthy. In the 19th century, the wealth was concentrated in Suzhou connected to Yangzhou along the Grand Canal. The wealthy bourgeois merchants located in this area were culturally nouveau, demanding that the local artisans provide them with a chance to emulate the literati and aristocratic figures to whom they aspired. Thus, art increasingly became a commercial activity. This is evident in several areas such as painting, porcelain, and glassware. A large group of glass snuff bottles survives along with very few objects which we can attribute to the commercial workshops of the 19th century. It is entirely likely that at this time, both good and bad were being produced simultaneously in large numbers by craftsmen at varying levels of competence.

By the last quarter of the 18th century and until the middle of the 19th century, glassmaking was prevalent not just in the imperial workshops but throughout the country in areas such as Boshan, Suzhou, and Yangzhou. It was revived again in the second half of the 19th century in Yangzhou. The largest group of Yangzhou School overlay bottles can be identified by its thin layer of single or multi-colored glass carved over a milk-white ground. Approximately one-third of these bottles have an inscription, seal, or the name of a pavilion carved on the bottle. The quality of this whole group is tremendously variable, from the poorest and meanest carving to the most elevated standard of decoration. As part of a commercial enterprise, this is understandable and today bottles must be judged as any work of art is, with a combination of its technical finesse and artistic endeavor.

In recent years dating of the whole group of Yangzhou School bottles has been reevaluated by Hugh Moss and Stuart Sargent based in part on the discovery that the name of a person carved on these bottles, Li Junting, was not a maker of bottles as was originally thought, but a collector of bottles who lived in the second half of the nineteenth century in the Yangzhou area. Just over ten percent of Yangzhou School bottles bear a cyclical date; sometimes alone, sometimes accompanying an artist's seal or inscription. Li Junting was a late nineteenth collector from Jingjiang, one of whose other given names was Weishi. This is known from snuff bottles carved with various combinations of names and dates, such as "Mr. Li of Jingjiang" with the seal 'Junting' or 'Weishi', or simply Li. Jingjiang is the old name for Zhenjiang, eight miles across the river from Yangzhou.

Both glass and enamel wares produced in southern China tend to depict naturalistic subject matters, evidence of the environment in which the pieces were made. Stylistically, Yangzhou School glass overlays are worlds away from the glass overlays of Beijing. The triple overlay carved bottles with fishermen on the river in sampans, or single overlays with cranes and bats are much less formalized than the classic subject matter of Beijing glass.

It is clear that even though they were made in the second half of the nineteenth century, the level of quality and sophistication of design is still there, albeit in a location far removed from the excesses of the late Qing court.

Enameling

There are many enamel on glass bottles that have merit other than those produced in the Palace Workshops. At some point in the Daoguang reign, *Guyue Xuan* marked copies of imperially produced enameled bottles began to be made outside of the Yuanming Yuan; some of them of very high quality. This seems logical given that the death of the Qianlong Emperor in 1799 would imply that there was no reason to make anything further for the Guyue Xuan, his retirement home, after that time.

During the Daoguang period, the atmosphere of the court was paling into insignificance compared to Daoguang's financial and political woes outside the palace. We know that the Emperor regularly bartered away imperial favors such as the right to use yellow, the imperial color, and it seems likely that, without potential retribution, an imperial mark such as *Guyue Xuan* would have then been eagerly taken up by enamellers outside the court, in both Beijing and Yangzhou.

Where were the other centers of enameling outside the Palace Workshops and when did they operate? Other known centers of enameling included Yangzhou, Guangzhou, and Yunnan, in addition to the private workshops in Beijing. The *Yangzhou Gazette (Hua Fang Lu)* mentions an enamel artist named Wang Shixing, who worked from sometime in the Yongzheng period into Qianlong's reign, that is to say in the mid-eighteenth century. The *Gazette* quotes as follows:

"He had many friends, and his fame spread throughout the land. In the Capital his fine craftsmanship was praised, this artist being known in Peking as the enamel-ware king."

This quote reveals much. Wang had 'many friends' (or clients) showing that even in the first half of the eighteenth century, he must have already been operating a lucrative commercial enterprise. This, in turn, suggests that enameled objects, including snuff bottles, were already popular outside the court. Wang's clients in Beijing (Peking) would have been exposed to his work, which must have been available for purchase in the city, as he was known there as 'the enamel-ware king'. This implies that in Beijing if a wealthy collector wanted a high-quality enamel piece, it could be commissioned from Wang Shixing in Yangzhou.

On what basis can enamel on glass bottles be attributed to Yangzhou? The bottles produced outside the palace have distinct characteristics. They are delicately designed with naturalistic subject matter, although some features, such as the neck borders and the side design, are reminiscent of palace work. The bottles are often separated into two scenes, sometimes by mask handles in a similar manner to glass overlay bottles. The enamels are thinner, and not "heaped", as would be expected from a commercial workshop where cost was a factor. The base marks on these bottles are either a *Guyue Xuan* mark in seal script (as opposed to regular script on palace enamel-wares) or they have a *Qianlong nian zhi* mark in seal script, generally written in a straight line instead of within a square.

50

清　乳白地疊套三色玻璃揚州工「赤壁泛舟」鼻煙壺

鼻煙壺揚州工，作扁瓶形。直口，溜肩，扁腹，腹下漸收，圈足。通體白地套紅、黃、綠三色玻璃，腹壁兩面浮雕湖光山水，此間白色背景作湖水留白，樹石、人物、烏鵲以綠色勾勒，遠空流雲襯以紅色，而一輪明月則巧妙以黃色彰顯。從明月、烏鵲與泛舟的線索，對照「月出於東山之上，徘徊於斗牛之間」的赤壁賦原文，可知此構圖為應為「赤壁泛舟」無疑。

1820-1880年
高：6.8厘米

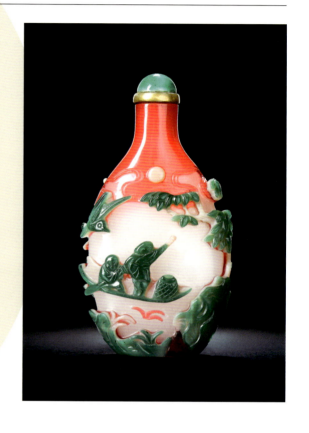

 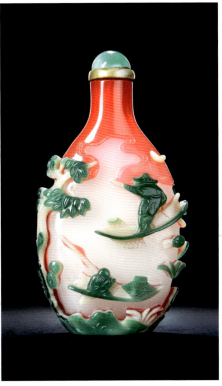 

A glass bottle, of slender, elongated, ovoid form with shoulders tapering to a cylindrical neck and with a neatly carved oval footrim; overlaid in green on yellow on pink, on a translucent milk-white ground; carved on one main side with a scene of a figure, one arm raised towards the sun, with his attendant and a wicker basket in a sampan on the river, a bird in flight beneath scrolling clouds, the grassy riverbank with trees and flowers issuing from rockwork; the reverse with a similar scene of two fishermen in boats on the river under a crescent moon and scrolling clouds beside the banks of a river.

Attributed to Yangzhou

1820-1880
Height: 6.8 cm

51

清　白地套紅色玻璃揚州工「延年益壽」鼻煙壺

鼻煙壺呈扁瓶形，為揚州工。直口，溜肩，扁腹，腹下漸收，
橢圓形圈足。通體半透明白地套紅色玻璃，兩面雕工，利用套
紅玻璃作點綴式勾紅處理。一面飾汀渚佇鶴，其右下方有「漁
珊」二字紅款。另一面則洞石聳立間，有兩隻蝙蝠盤旋上下，
洞石上端並署有「延年益壽」四字橫書篆體款。

1820-1880年
高：5.8 厘米

A glass bottle, of flattened, rounded form with shoulders tapering to a cylindrical neck, and with a neatly carved oval footrim; overlaid in red on a milk-white ground; carved on one main side with a red-crested crane clutching a branch of *lingzhi* in its beak, standing on one leg on a rock by a grassy bank, a seal to one side reading "Yu Shan"; the reverse with two bats flying above a convoluted rock rising from waves; a four-character inscription to one side reading "wishes for longevity in life."

Attributed to Yangzhou

1820-1880
Height: 5.8 cm

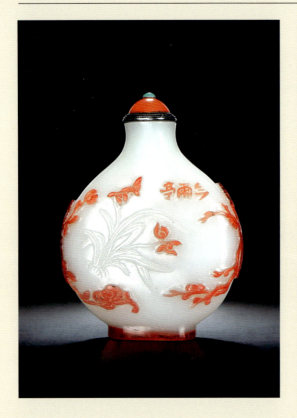
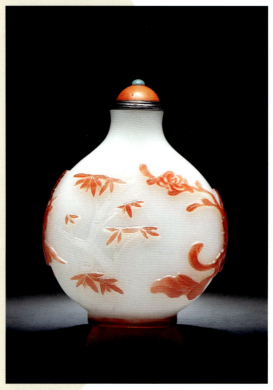

52

清　白地套紅色玻璃揚州工「梅蘭竹菊」鼻煙壺

鼻煙壺呈扁瓶形。直口，溜肩，廣腹，腹下漸收，橢圓形圈
足。通體半透明白地套紅色玻璃，兩側面以紅色顯花分別飾
以梅菊花卉，腹壁兩面以套紅玻璃重點勾勒，一面浮雕修竹斜
倚，另一面則蘭葉朵花兀自綻放，右上方並署有「今雨亭」三
字款。

是件鼻煙壺用色清雅，恰如其分的構圖用心，剛好符合梅蘭竹
菊四君子的高貴文人特色。

1820-1880年
高：5.9 厘米

A glass bottle, of flattened, rounded form with shoulders tapering to a cylindrical neck with a slightly everted mouth, and with a neatly carved oval footrim; overlaid in red on a milk-white ground; carved on one main side with a natural scene of flowering lilies issuing from rockwork beneath a three-character inscription reading "Pavilion of Cloud and Rain"; the reverse carved with bamboo issuing from rockwork; the narrow sides each carved with leafy flowering prunus branches.

Attributed to Yangzhou

1820-1880
Height: 5.9 cm

53

清　白地套藍色玻璃揚州工「三秋圖」鼻煙壺

鼻煙壺作柳葉瓶式。敞口，短頸，豐肩，肩下削瘦至足，圈足，器身細長，形似柳葉，故又有「美人肩」之稱。通體白色地套藍色玻璃，腹壁以藍色顯花，分別飾有洞石、蘭花、菊花、桂樹、鳳凰與蝙蝠等，又頸肩一處署有「三秋圖」三字篆書款。

據悉，古人將農曆的七、八、九月，分別稱為孟秋、仲秋、季秋，合稱三秋。故畫家常以秋天可見之桂花、菊花、禽鳥等圖像，作為三秋圖的題材內容。

1820-1880年
高：7.7 厘米

A glass bottle, of *meiping* form with shoulders tapering to a cylindrical neck with a slightly everted mouth, and with a neatly carved oval footrim; overlaid in blue on a milk-white ground; continuously carved with a natural scene of long-tailed birds and bats in flight above flowering lilies, leafy chrysanthemums and a gnarly tree issuing from convoluted rockwork, the shoulders with a three-character inscription reading "Picture of Autumn."

Attributed to Yangzhou

1820-1880
Height: 7.7 cm

54

清　黃地疊套雙色玻璃揚州工「海屋添籌」鼻煙壺

鼻煙壺呈扁瓶形。直口，溜肩，深腹，腹下近底部急收，橢圓形圈足。通體黃色地套紅、綠色玻璃，腹壁兩面做通景式構圖，波滔洶湧的大壑上矗立一樓閣，樓閣綠瓦紅窗，一派蓬島華屋的景色，而華屋的上空群鶴翔飛，恰恰是「海屋添籌」的典型構圖意象。

1820-1880年
高：7.1 厘米

A glass bottle, of slender, elongated, ovoid form with shoulders tapering to a cylindrical neck with everted mouth, and with a neatly carved oval footrim; overlaid in cinnabar-red on green on a caramel-colored ground; carved on one main side with a scene of two cranes in flight, one with a rod in its beak, above a pavilion beside a lake, nestled in a mountainous landscape, all under scrolling clouds with the sun high in the sky, a two character seal to one side; the reverse with three cranes and a bat in flight below scrolling clouds and above the sun rising from waves beside a rocky bank.

Attributed to Yangzhou

1820-1880
Height: 7.1 cm

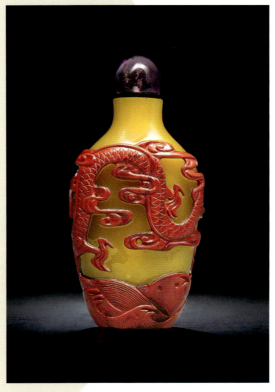

55

清　黃套漆紅色玻璃「魚躍龍門」鼻煙壺

鼻煙壺呈扁瓶形。直口，溜肩，深腹，腹下漸收，橢圓形圈足。通體黃色地套漆紅色玻璃，所套漆紅料甚厚，復以剔地技法，高浮雕一尾呈跳躍狀的鯉魚正奮力躍出海面，而海平面上一尾做盤繞狀的遊龍，恰與頭鬣長角的鯉魚目光交接。據此演繹，一幅力爭上游的「魚躍龍門」圖像，也就於焉誕生了。

1820-1880年
高：6.2 厘米

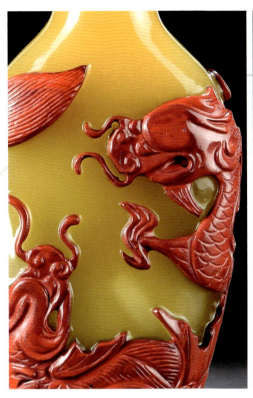

A glass bottle, of slender, elongated, ovoid form with shoulders tapering to a cylindrical neck with slightly everted mouth, and with a neatly carved oval foot; overlaid in cinnabar-red on a caramel-colored ground; continuously carved with a scene of a coiling scaly dragon flying though the sky, a second dragon rising from frothy waves below.

Attributed to Yangzhou

1820-1880
Height: 6.2 cm

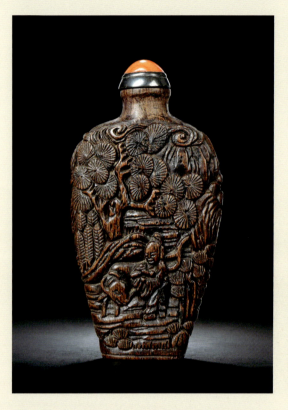

56

清　沉香木雕「歸田耕讀」鼻煙壺

鼻煙壺沉香木雕成。呈扁瓶形。唇口，短頸，豐肩，扁腹，腹下漸收，橢圓形圈足。兩面雕工，皆以減地技法，雕飾兩組既可獨立又能相互聯結的通景式山水人物圖。其中一面雕竹石桐蔭旁，一著朝服的文士正展卷閱讀；另一面則松下水田間一人似趕牛拉犁辛勤耕作。結合兩組畫面，所謂「歸田耕讀」的退隱文人意象，也就自然呈現眼前了。

1800-1900年
高：7.2 厘米

An aloes wood (*chenxiangmu*) bottle, of flattened, *meiping* form with shoulders sloping to a cylindrical neck with straightened mouth; carved with a scene of an ox herder and his ox in a rocky mountainous landscape surrounded by a forest of pine and other trees; the reverse with a similar scene with a sage seated on a rock, reading a book; all under scrolling clouds.

Attributed to Guangzhou

1800-1900
Height: 7.2 cm

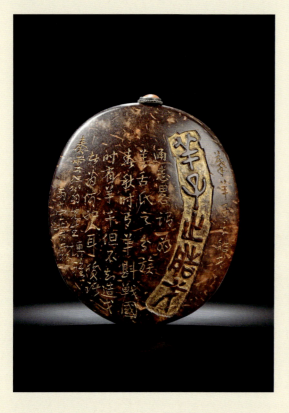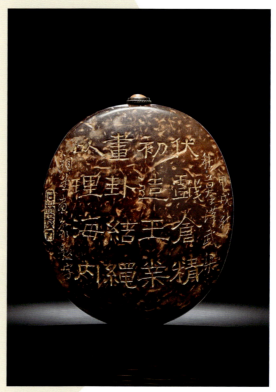

57

清　椰殼雕摹古金石銘文鼻煙壺

鼻煙壺兩件弧面椰殼拼合而成，略成圓形卵石狀，通體呈深紫色，兩面雕飾填金摹古金石銘文。其中一面鐫隸書：「伏羲倉精，初造王業。畫卦結繩，以理海內。」十六字銘。兩邊署「甲戌新秋，摹漢武梁祠堂畫象題字」。末鐫「石林後人」四字長方印。另一面刻（金文）五字「羊子之造戈」。「摹羊子之造戈，《通志》署謂為：羊舌氏之分族，春秋時有羊斟，戰國時有羊千，但不知造戈者為何如人耳。質諸奏雲仁翁先生博雅，雨亭葉霖。」

1874年秋
高：6厘米

一面鐫隸書十六字銘：

「伏羲蒼精，初造王業。畫卦結繩，以理海內。」

兩邊署：

「甲戌新秋，摹漢武梁祠堂畫象題字。」「石林後人」

末鐫四字長方印：

另一面刻（金文）五字：

「羊子之造戈」。「摹羊子之造戈，《通志》署謂為：羊舌氏之分族，春秋時有羊斟，戰國時有羊千，但不知造戈者為何如人耳。質諸奏雲仁翁先生博雅，雨亭葉霖。」

A coconut bottle, of circular shape, formed from two convex segments, well patinated and engraved on each main side with lengthy inscriptions; one side with sixteen characters in large clerical script:

"When Fuxi, who is aged but clear-sighted, first established himself as king, he painted the Eight Trigrams [for divination] and tied knots in ropes [for record-keeping], [the first emperors] governed the entire country."

Followed by:

"Early autumn of the *Jiaxu* Year, copying the inscription for the illustration [of Fuxi and Nuwa] at the Wu Liang Shrine of the Han."

A rectangular seal with four characters: "Descendant of Shilin" [lit. Stone Forest].

The reverse with:

"The dagger made by Yangzi,

The [Southern Song Dynasty] Comprehensive Records lists Yangzi as branch of the Yangshe family.

During the Spring and Autumn periods there was Yang Zhen, and the Warring States period there was Yang Qian,

It is unknown who made this dagger, for the knowledgeable and elegant Zhouyun Renwing, by Yelin of Yuting [Rain Pavilion]."

Attributed to Guangzhou

Autumn, 1874
Height: 6 cm

北京

料器

根據墓地考古發掘與早期文獻記載，我們可知料器（玻璃）早在公元前五世紀便傳入中國。早期料器有珠子、劍飾和璧等。自始，料器生產逐漸發展到中國各地。公元一世紀，中國工匠開始運用玻璃吹製技術、鐵桿取熔融玻璃技術。吹製玻璃的引入，對於各地區文化來說都是一大創新，它使玻璃生產得以擴大規模，降低成本，研發新品。雖然我們找不到有關明代玻璃產地的資料，但是毫無疑問，玻璃生產工藝在明代（1368-1644年）得到提升，為其於清代跳躍性發展做好準備。料器有四大產地：博山、廣州、蘇州和北京，它們僅僅能為我們提供早期玻璃工藝發展的基本信息。

明代，博山的玻璃作坊在顏神鎮，當地原材料豐富，所產料器「乾淨、光滑、甜美」。孫廷銓記載清初博山所製玻璃十分名貴，有藍色玻璃扇頁、陳設燈籠、鏡子等。1640-1641年間，長江以北地區出現乾旱，導致當地百分之九十的工匠死亡，極大影響了玻璃生產。1982年10月27日，山東省淄博市博物館畢思良先生在博山老城區考古發現了一處古代玻璃作坊遺址。這是首次在中國境內發現元末明初玻璃作坊的遺址，從遺址挖掘出來的瓷器、錢幣以及玻璃碎片可相互驗證年代。

中國南方廣州一帶的玻璃生產亦十分有名。作為一處活躍的對外貿易港口，廣州深深受到了西洋進口商品的影響，當地的玻璃工匠吸收了穆斯林和歐洲玻璃工藝。

關於蘇州玻璃製造的文獻不多。梁同書所記：「蘇鑄者不如廣鑄。」

現在我們還不清楚北京從什麼時候開始玻璃的商業生產。考慮到北京是三朝古都，加上玻璃生產由宮廷掌控，北京應當較早便有玻璃生產。北京加工的玻璃亦稱「料器」，意指用山東所產玻璃製作的器物。這個稱號乃博山玻璃工匠所取，後於北京被廣泛使用。北京並無生產玻璃物料，而是從其他地方購買玻璃錠和玻璃原條等半成品，然後重新加熱吹製成最終產品。乾隆年間，內廷與宮外富裕階層流行吸食鼻煙，當時有三大作坊—辛家、勒家和袁家，它們競相爭奪鼻煙壺市場。分辨某一鼻煙壺出自哪家之手，既艱難又有趣。因此，多年來流傳了很多有關他們作品的故事。

十九世紀六十年代的文獻記載：「辛家套料鼻煙壺以珍珠著稱，質量清靈秀潔。」

文獻提及，袁家套料鼻煙壺與辛家相似。

有關勒家的文獻記載：「以藕粉色地取勝，質如冰雪。顏色運用超凡，紅、紫、天藍、翠藍等色料相間，自然流淌。」但我們無法明確，此處「藕粉色地」是指乳白色地還是雪霏地。我們可知的是，此三家在乾隆時期生產套料鼻煙壺，並在十九世紀六十年代前便赫赫有名。

內畫

丁尚庚（1865-1935年），字二仲，号潞河。所製鼻煙壺多落「二仲」款以及其特有的紅印。丁尚庚是一個畫家、書法家、篆刻家、竹刻家，最重要的，他是一名十九世紀非常重要的鼻煙壺內畫家，活跃于京城內畫商業圈，崇尚周樂元等前人風格。其他北京著名內畫家有馬少宣和葉仲三。

自1893年起，丁二仲在北京創作內畫器物，直至八國聯軍進攻北京，其父在與八國聯軍的衝突中死亡，丁二仲和母親隨後搬往南京。在他兩件內畫鼻煙壺作品上，丁二仲描繪了他京中作坊附近區域「宣南」—宣武門南邊，宣武門是北京西南邊的老城門。這裡也是周樂元以及其他多位內畫藝人作坊所在。有意思的是，該地區旁邊便是一個古玩市場，古董商們在此交易絲綢之路上所尋獲的各式器物。

丁二仲是名副其實的內畫大師，雖然他和周樂元均從事商業活動，但他有其學術理想，並精通書畫和詩詞兩項中國傳統藝術。這體現在其所描繪的題材與所題的詩詞上。

最初，丁二仲所繪內畫鼻煙壺多模仿周樂元的題材，但並非完全複製。丁二仲可能與周樂元相識，和葉仲三不同，他們均不是按書畫樣。其繪畫別具一格，並能十分精巧地體現在其作品上。考慮到鼻煙壺尺寸之小，筆觸更顯巧妙。二十世紀初，丁二仲逐漸減少製作鼻煙壺，轉而創作其他器物如扇子和印章。約在1914年後，完全停止了繪製內畫鼻煙壺。

料胎畫琺瑯

葉菶祺(1908-1974年)，雖然葉菶祺是內畫作坊「杏林齋」一員，但他最為人樂道的是其料胎畫琺瑯工藝。本書收藏系列中所藏的葉菶祺製鼻煙壺展示了其最高水平，光影明暗變化細膩，繪畫精巧，可與十八世紀宮廷料胎畫琺瑯相比。當然，這可能與葉菶祺在當學徒時常進出宮廷有關。葉菶祺是葉仲三第三子，雖然他亦研習內畫，但不及其父親與兩位兄長。葉菶祺跟隨父親葉仲三學習畫琺瑯，而葉仲三則是受藝於葉菶祺祖父。我們很難從存世的畫琺瑯鼻煙壺中分辨出哪件屬葉仲三親筆，因此，我們把這些鼻煙壺均認定為葉菶祺所製。

我們所能掌握的大部分關於葉菶祺的資料來自三十多年前，1974年，他與莫仕撝(Hugh Moss) 的對話。雖然當時葉先生年事已高，但莫仕撝還年輕，因此他有幸把這些珍貴信息記錄下來。

「杏林齋」所用的窯口是一個家庭式小窯，每次只能燒製一件作品。這是一個使用備長炭為燃料的黏土窯，加上冷卻過程，每次燒造時間約2小時。這種燒造無法精確控制成品效果，葉菶祺估計僅有30%的機率最終燒製成功。每件作品，包括鼻煙壺、迷你花瓶、筆洗以及其他文房珍玩，需在黑彩線描的基礎上添加彩料，因此需要經歷起碼四次入窯燒製。

在正式從藝前，葉菶祺進行了長達三年的學習（約在1920年前後）。他告訴莫仕撝，他最初是用破碎的玻璃進行練習，直至1924年成功繪製首件正式作品。其後不斷探索，於1933-1943年間形成個人風格，創作出一批精品。1949年後，雖然葉菶祺向王習三（後來的內畫大師）傳授畫琺瑯工藝，但此時葉菶祺本人鮮有繪製。葉菶祺所製鼻煙壺均做商業用途，出售給北京城裡的經銷商，經銷商將這些鼻煙壺當十八世紀的原作出售。因葉菶祺的精品絲毫不輸原作，以至於我們現在仍不時將二者混淆。可是，皆因他僅能在每次參觀故宮博物院後，憑記憶模仿宮中的原作，他的作品和原作在細節上有所不同。

葉菶祺所用的料胎來自起碼兩個不同渠道。難得的是，他能獲取一些老胎進行創作。與此同時，在京城有一位玻璃工匠，人稱料壺周，長年為葉菶祺供應素胎料壺。我們對其所知甚少，僅知道他居住在崇文門外，使用自家小窯燒造各式玻璃器皿，如鼻煙壺。他也製作仿古料器，顏色多樣，亦有套色作品，收有一名學生，孫氏，其詳細資料如今已無法追溯，可能已經故去。

葉葊祺的作品，使用堆填法，即用大量厚重的粉彩彩料層層堆疊而成，形成一種立體效果，色彩鮮明（雖然沒有王習三的顏色明亮）。底用藍料堆填「乾隆年製」四字款、「乾隆」二字款、或十分稀有的「古月軒」款。此工藝雖然需要多重燒製，卻似乎避免了十八世紀琺瑯工藝帶縮釉點的缺陷。

葉葊祺的代表作常繪有流暢的花鳥紋樣，並配以複雜帶狀圖案。葉葊祺很少在其作品上繪製風景，據說約有十件，個別仿抱子石開光形制的宮廷樣式。

近日，莫仕爲重新整理了其早年研究，根據他與葉葊祺的訪談，提出了幾個有趣的問題。雖然葉葊祺聲稱他在故宮博物院學習四年後，於1924年開始創作用於商業用途的畫琺瑯作品，但故宮博物院直到1925年10月才對外開放。因此，莫仕爲認為，葉葊祺在1924年前並沒有機會仿製宮廷料胎畫琺瑯鼻煙壺，這些他聲稱是自己作品的鼻煙壺實際產於十八世紀。據莫仕爲所說，其中包括了原葛氏所藏於1921-1924年間購於北京的鼻煙壺。假如莫仕爲觀點成立，那麼還有另外一種可能。葛氏所藏的宮廷料胎畫琺瑯鼻煙壺證實了當時這些御製鼻煙壺從宮中流出，流入北京的古玩商手中，再被出售。與此同時，古玩商從葉葊祺處以四十大元購買仿品，後以兩千大元的價格當成原作出售。假設這些古玩商手中有宮廷原作，葉葊祺極有可能看到了這些作品，並受邀進行仿製。葉葊祺可能為了面子，並沒有告訴莫仕爲真實情況，而說他去了故宮博物院參觀並模仿這些宮廷鼻煙壺。

BEIJING

Glass

A combination of archaeological tomb excavations and early Chinese writings tells that glass has been present in China from around the fifth century B.C. Early period objects included beads, sword ornaments, and *bi* discs. This was an ongoing tradition spreading the manufacture of glass throughout the land. Since the first century A.D. techniques such as glass-blowing and the 'pontil' technique were in use. In any culture the introduction of blown glass would have been an important innovation, enabling production to increase, cost to decrease, and form to develop. However, it was during the Ming dynasty (1368-1644) that advances were made which paved the way for a dramatic improvement in manufacture in the Qing dynasty (1644-1912); although there is scant evidence relating to the sites of glass production during this dynasty. Four sites – Boshan, Guangzhou, Suzhou, and Beijing provide us with only threadbare information about the early development of glass.

During the Ming dynasty, the Boshan glassworks located at Yanshen were rich in raw materials and produced glass which according to one source was 'clear, smooth and lovely.' Sun Tingquan stated that during the early Qing dynasty the goods from Boshan were 'luxury articles' such as blue window blinds, decorated lanterns, and mirrors. This was despite a drought in the area north of the Yangtze River in 1640-41 that had seriously damaged glass production and had caused the death of ninety percent of the workers there. On 27th October 1982, Bi Siliang of the Zibo Municipal Museum, Shandong uncovered the remains of an ancient glass factory in the old town area of Boshan. This was the first discovery of a glasshouse in China and can be conservatively dated to the late Yuan/early Ming period. Evidence of ceramics, coins, and glass shards on the site has corroborated this information.

The southeast of China around Guangzhou was also known for its glass production. As a thriving foreign trade port, it was also the place where the influences of Western imports would have been strongest and where the techniques of Islamic and European glass would have been acquired by the Chinese glassmakers.

Glassmaking in Suzhou is not extensively recorded. According to Liang Tongshu, 'The glass objects made by the people of Suzhou during the Qing dynasty were even poorer in quality than those made by the people of Guangzhou.'

It is still not clear when Beijing's commercial glass production began. Given that Beijing was the capital of the last three dynasties and that glass production was a centralized process it is likely that it commenced relatively early. Glass crafted in Beijing was termed *Liao qi* meaning objects fashioned from glass made in Shandong. This was the name given by the glassmakers of Boshan to glass which was subsequently used in Beijing. There was no initial manufacturing process of glass from raw materials in Beijing; it was transported into the area as ingots or blocks which were then reheated and blown to make the finished product. During the reign of Qianlong when snuff taking was fashionable both at court and with the wealthy, there was keen competition between three studios for the production of snuff bottles - the Xin family, the Le family, and the Yuan family. Attributions of individual bottles to these families is a tenuous though appealing notion. As such the stories of their work have been embellished over the years. Quotes translated from a text of the 1860s state:

'The Xin family overlays are the most cleanly done and as their colors are made out of crushed gems, the luster dazzles the eye.'

Of the Yuan family overlays, the text notes that they are similar to the Xin family examples. A reference to the Le family states:

'These have a 'lotus-powder ground' as white as frozen snow. The way that the colors are arranged is also quite extraordinary with red, purple, sky-blue, and kingfisher-blue alternating one with the other in a natural fashion.'

However, it is not clear whether 'lotus powder ground' refers to an opaque milk-white ground or a 'snowflake' ground. All that can be assumed is that three families were making fine overlay snuff bottles in the Qianlong period who were famous by the 1860s.

Inside Painted

Ding Erzhong (1865-1935)

Erzhong is the personal name of Ding Shanyu (1865-1935) whose art name was *Luhe*. Most of his bottles are signed with simply the personal name, Erzhong with his distinctive red seal. Ding was a painter, a calligrapher, a seal carver, a bamboo carver but first and foremost, a painter of snuff bottles in the late nineteenth century, and as such was a part of the commercial world of the Beijing inside painted school, following in the tradition of artists such as Zhou Leyuan. Other well-known artists in Beijing included Ma Shaoxuan and Ye Zhongsan.

Ding worked in Beijing from 1893 until he moved to Nanjing with his mother, after his father was killed in the fighting with the Allied Forces when they marched on the city. On two of his bottles, Ding identifies the area of Beijing where he worked which was known as Xuannan, south of the *Xuanwu men*, one of the gates to the old city in the southwest of Beijing. This is also where Zhou Leyuan had his studio, as did several other inside-painted artists that worked in the city. Interestingly, this area was next to the antique market where the dealers plied their trade with wares found along the Silk Road.

Ding Erzhong is justifiably recognized as one of the great masters of the inside painting world and whilst he was commercial, like Zhou Leyuan, he also held some scholarly ideals and was knowledgeable in calligraphy and poetry, two of the 'high arts' of China. This is reflected in the subject matter of his painting and the inscriptions in his sure hand that accompany them.

Initially, Ding worked painting inside snuff bottles, at times copying the subject matter of Zhou Leyuan, although never with entirely the same design. Like Zhou, whom he may have known, he did not work from a design book as Ye Zhongsan so clearly did. His painting is always unique and faultlessly executed in his own style. Considering the restriction of the size of a snuff bottle, his brushwork is masterly. After the first years of the twentieth century Ding's snuff bottle output wound down and he turned to produce other items such as fans and seals. After 1914, it appears that Ding had ceased painting inside bottles entirely.

Enamel On Glass
Ye Bengqi (1908-1974)
Although part of the inside painting studio known as the Apricot Grove Studio, Ye Bengqi is perhaps best known for his enameling skills. The bottle by Ye Bengqi in this collection shows the artist at his best; with its delicate shading and fine painting, it is comparable to an eighteenth-century imperial enamel on glass bottle. The reason for this, of course, lies in the proximity of Ye Bengqi to the palace during his training. Ye Bengqi was the third son of Ye Zhongsan and, although he learned the skill of inside painting, he was already fourth in line behind his father and his two older brothers. Ye Bengqi was taught enameling by his father, Ye Zhongsan, who in turn was apparently taught the art by his grandfather. It is not possible to separate the extant bottles enameled by Ye Zhongsan, and as a consequence, bottles of this period of enameling are all attributed to Ye Bengqi.

Much of the information we have about Ye Bengqi comes from a series of interviews with him by Hugh Moss in 1974, over thirty years ago. Although Ye was an older man at this point, Moss was still relatively young and fortunately, he documented the information given to him by Ye.

The kiln used at the Apricot Grove Studio was a small family-run kiln that took only one object at a time. It was a clay-lined kiln and used "white" charcoal for the firing, which took an average of two hours including a cooling period. It was not scientifically controlled and Ye estimated that only 30% of his pieces were successful. Each object, which included, in addition to snuff bottles, miniature vases, brush washers and other small scholars' works of art, needed to be fired at least four times as enamel colors were added to the initial design sketched in black enamel.

Ye Bengqi studied for at least three years (around 1920) before he began enameling bottles. He told Moss that he thought his first "real" enamel bottle was made around 1924 after using chipped or broken glass bottles to practice on. He developed his art over the next few years reaching a peak in quality between 1933 and 1943 when his best works were produced. After 1949, he did very little enameling, although he was responsible for teaching the art to his student, Wang Xisan, who became a master in his own right. The bottles that Ye Bengqi produced were made for commercial purposes and were sold to Beijing dealers, who in turn sold them as eighteenth-century palace originals. This has led to some confusion today as some of Ye Bengqi's copies are as good as the originals. However, his copies are never exact as he had to sketch from memory after he visited the Palace Museum.

The milk-white glass bottles that Ye Bengqi used came from at least two known sources. More rarely, he was able to find older blanks that could be used for enameling. There was also a glassmaker in Beijing known as 'Glass Bottle Zhou' (Zhou Liaohu) who produced blanks for Ye Bengqi. Very little is known of him except that he lived in Beijing outside the Zhongwen Gate and used his private kiln for making glass objects, including snuff bottles. He also copied antique glass, in various colors, including overlay pieces. One of Zhou's students was named Sun, who cannot be traced and would now be deceased.

The majority of Ye's works are produced using the heaping method, with layers of thick opaque enamels in a *famille-rose* palette, resulting in a more three-dimensional decoration which was very vivid in tone (although not as bright as Wang Xisan's work). The base mark was executed as either a "heaped" four-character *Qianlong nian zhi* mark or a two-character *Qianlong* mark, or very rarely a *Guyue Xuan* mark, all in blue enamel. The heaping method, with its multiple firings, seemed to avoid the pitting evident on eighteenth-century enamels.

Ye's finest works are of flowing bird and flower designs with intricately worked borders. Very occasionally, Ye Bengqi also did landscapes, allegedly about ten, some with "puddingstone" marbled borders, again in imitation of the palace style.

Moss's recent re-evaluation of his earlier research raises some interesting questions relating to his series of interviews with Ye Bengqi. Although Ye claimed that he started enameling commercially in 1924 after studying at the Palace Museum for four years, the museum was not open to the public until October 1925. Moss concludes, therefore, that Ye Bengqi had, in effect, no "imperial" enamels on glass to copy in 1924 and that it was likely that some bottles claimed by Ye Bengqi as his own, are in fact, original eighteenth-century enamels. This, according to Moss, includes some bottles from the Ko Collection which were purchased in Beijing between 1921 and 1924. While this conclusion is possible, there is another viable scenario. The "imperial" enamels from the Ko Collection purchased in Beijing confirm the fact that bottles were being removed from the palace around this time and passed to dealers in Beijing who were selling them. These were the same dealers who were buying Ye's copies for forty yuan and selling them also as palace originals for two thousand yuan. If these dealers had original "palace" bottles, it is entirely likely that Ye Bengqi would have been shown them and even be asked by the dealers to copy them. Ye Bengqi may not have wanted to reveal this to Moss to save face and may have simply stated that he had been going into the Museum to copy the bottles.

清　透明綠色玻璃冬梅春蘭鼻煙壺

玻璃鼻煙壺，作扁瓶形。直口，溜肩，垂腹，腹下漸收，橢圓形圈足。通體透明綠色玻璃，玻璃內滿布氣泡，腹壁兩面雕工。一面飾淺浮雕春蘭，另一面飾冬梅，蘭梅之間有彩蝶翩翩飛舞。全器因綠色氣泡掩映而顯得幽雅深邃，此外梅蘭花卉的倩影勾勒，也有書畫小品的筆墨韻致。

1750-1820年
高：6.5 厘米

A glass bottle, of flattened teardrop form, with shoulders sloping to a cylindrical neck, and with a neatly carved oval footrim; the Westlake-green glass suffused with bubbles and carved on each main side with flowering lilies.

Attributed to Beijing

1750-1820
Height: 6.5 cm

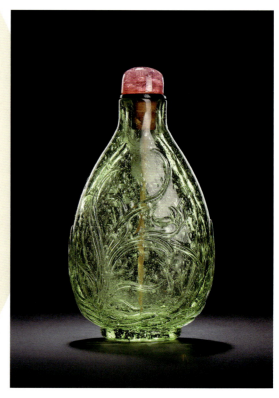

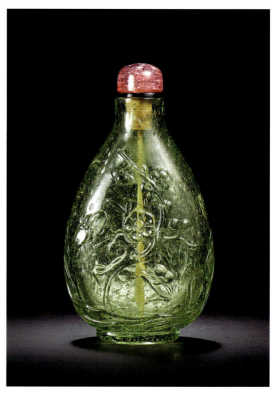

59

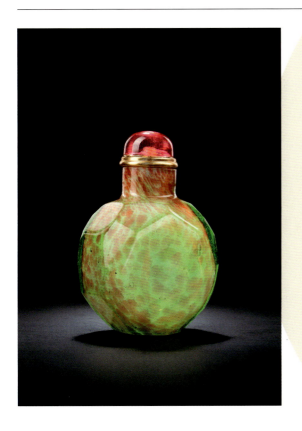

清　透明綠色玻璃攪斑紅色磨稜八角鼻煙壺

玻璃鼻煙壺，作八角扁瓶形。直口，平底。通體涅白色地套攪斑紅、透明綠色玻璃，三層疊套的攪色玻璃工藝已屬相當難能可貴，全器復以磨花技術，將壺體、腹壁磨切成規律的八角幾何形，確是一件費工耗時且視覺優美的箇中精品。

1750-1800年
高：4.5 厘米

A glass bottle, of small octagonal faceted form, with a cylindrical neck, and a neatly carved flat foot, each main side with a faceted central panel bordered by multi-facets; with dappled pink glass swirls sandwiched between an outer layer of transparent green glass suffused with bubbles, and an inner layer of opalescent white glass.

Attributed to Beijing

1750-1800
Height: 4.5 cm

60

清　珍珠地套紅玻璃竹石花卉鼻煙壺

玻璃鼻煙壺，作扁瓶形。直口，溜肩，腹下漸收，橢圓形圈足。通體無色透明珍珠地套紅色玻璃，腹壁兩面雕工，皆以紅色顯花，一面飾洞石芝草上有梅枝斜出，另一面則以修竹的意象，將竹葉巧妙排列成文字，曰「亭有餘香」四字。

全器色彩鮮活，紋樣線條流暢，是一件能讓人有意外驚喜的掌中雅物。

1750-1800年
高：6.4 厘米

A glass bottle, of flattened, rounded form with shoulders tapering to a cylindrical neck and with a neatly carved oval footrim; overlaid in red on a snowflake ground; carved on one main side with rockwork from which branches of bamboo grow, in a design resembling calligraphy reading:

"The strokes shaped like bamboo leaves, fragrance lingers in the pavilion."

the reverse with a scene of a blossoming prunus branch growing from rockwork beside *lingzhi,* all in the shade of a pine tree; the two narrow sides with rockwork.

Attributed to Beijing

1750-1800
Height: 6.4 cm

意象文字：「亭有餘香」

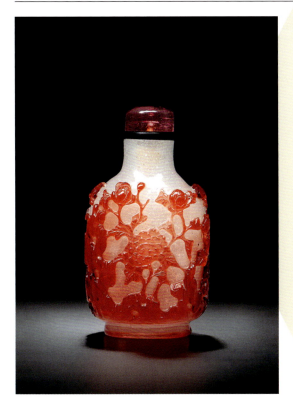

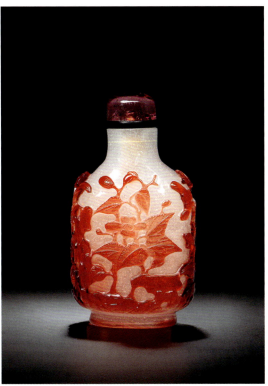

清　珍珠地套紅玻璃「玉堂富貴」鼻煙壺

玻璃鼻煙壺，呈扁瓶形。直口，深腹，腹下急收，橢圓形圈足。通體無色透明珍珠地套紅色玻璃，腹壁以剔地技法，高浮雕草蟲花卉。一面湖石飾折枝牡丹，另一面則是折枝海棠，兩側面牡丹上有蝴蝶，海棠上有蜻蜓。蝴蝶、蜻蜓俱是美好的意象，連結在海棠、牡丹的「玉堂富貴」中，自然沒有絲毫違和感。

1750-1800年
高：5.2 厘米

A glass bottle, of rectangular form with shoulders tapering to a cylindrical neck and with a neatly carved slightly splayed, oval footrim; overlaid in red on a snowflake ground; carved continuously with serrated rockwork with leafy flowering shrubs on the two main sides.

Attributed to Beijing

1750-1800
Height: 5.2 cm

62

清　珍珠地套紅玻璃「一團和氣」鼻煙壺

玻璃鼻煙壺。直口，短頸，溜肩，腹下漸收，橢圓形圈足。通體無色透明珍珠地套紅色玻璃，腹壁兩面以紅色顯花做圓形開光，開光內淺浮雕體態渾圓的童子，童子雙手持拿一卷署有「一團和氣」的橫聯，兩肩側面飾一對淺浮雕獸首銜環耳。全器用色紅艷討喜，予人和諧安康的美好感受。

1750-1800年
高：5.5 厘米

A glass bottle, of flattened, rounded form with shoulders tapering to a cylindrical neck with slightly everted mouth, and with a neatly carved oval footrim; overlaid in red on a snowflake ground; carved on each main side within a circular red panel with a happy boy in loose flowing robes, holding a banner incised with a four-character inscription reading: "A prevailing mood of harmony," the shoulders with mock mask and ring handles.

Attributed to Beijing

1750-1800
Height: 5.5 cm

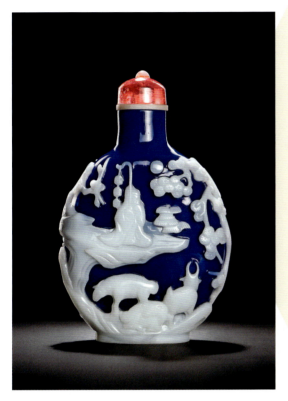

清　藍色地套白色玻璃人物故事鼻煙壺

玻璃鼻煙壺，作扁瓶形。直口，短頸，溜肩，腹下漸收，橢圓形圈足。通體不透明藍色地套白色玻璃，腹壁兩面以白色顯花，分別雕飾人物故事圖。一面浮雕身著厚袍的倚杖老翁與群羊意象，自然是「蘇武牧羊」圖，另一面則梅枝斜出下，有一文士騎驢緩行，那應該是表現孟浩然灞橋覓詩之「踏雪尋梅」的場景了。

1750-1820年
高：6.3 厘米

A glass bottle, of flattened, rounded form with shoulders tapering to a cylindrical neck, and with a neatly carved oval footrim; overlaid in white on an opaque cobalt-blue ground; carved on one main side with a goat herder seated on a rocky outcrop tending to his goats grazing below him, set in a mountainous landscape bordered by pine trees and under a sun high in the sky; the reverse with Meng Haoran astride his mule travelling with his attendant who carries a prunus branch over his shoulder, a blossoming prunus tree framing the scene.

Attributed to Beijing

1750-1820
Height: 6.3 cm

清　黃地套藍色玻璃花卉禽蟲鼻煙壺

玻璃鼻煙壺，作圓罐形。唇口，深腹，圈足。通體不透明
黃色地套藍色玻璃，以藍色顯花，雕飾折枝梅花、海棠、
蘭花、水仙、文竹以及蝙蝠與蜜蜂等，全器以各種寓意吉
祥的花卉禽蟲，營造繽紛的熱鬧氣息。又黃套藍色玻璃鼻
煙壺，在留存數量上原屬罕見，故其難能可貴的藝術價值
也就不在話下了。

1750-1800年
高：7.4 厘米

A glass bottle, of slender, elongated ovoid form with shoulders tapering to a cylindrical neck with everted mouth, and with a neatly carved oval footrim; overlaid in cobalt-blue on an opaque yellow ground; carved on one main side with a flowering peony between a bat and a bee, the reverse with a blossoming prunus branch between a bat and *lingzhi*; the two narrow sides carved with flowering peonies; the mouth encircled with a blue collar.

Attributed to Beijing

1750-1800
Height: 7.4 cm

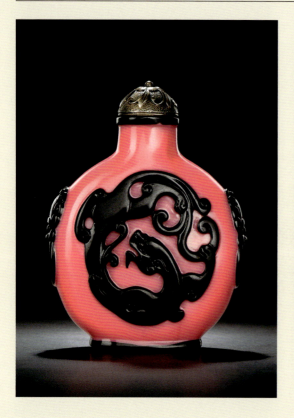

65

清　胭脂地套黑色玻璃團螭紋鼻煙壺

玻璃鼻煙壺，呈扁瓶形。直口，短頸，溜肩，腹下漸收，橢圓形圈足。通體不透明胭脂紅地套黑色玻璃，以黑色顯花於兩側壁貼飾浮雕獸首銜環耳，腹壁兩面，一面飾線條流轉的團螭紋，另一面以凸弦紋圍繞成圓形開光，開光內填飾三行篆書，曰「雲行雨施，萬國咸寧」八字。末署「庶」、「齋」二字印章款。

是件鼻煙壺配色大膽，能奪人眼球，所飾圖像紋樣瑰麗工整，亦是一件不可多得的精美雅物。

1750-1800年
高：6 厘米

圓形開光內浮雕八字：

「雲行雨施，萬國咸寧」

末署二字印章款：

「庶」、「齋」

A glass bottle, of flattened, rounded form with shoulders tapering to a cylindrical neck, and with a neatly carved oval footrim; overlaid in black on an opaque pink ground; carved on one main side with a roundel encircling an eight-character inscription reading:

"The clouds move, spreading the rain, giving peace to the ten-thousand nations."

followed by two seals 'Shu' and 'Zhai'; the reverse carved with a coiling *chilong* forming a circular medallion; the shoulders carved with mock mask and ring handles.

Attributed to Beijing

1750-1800
Height: 6 cm

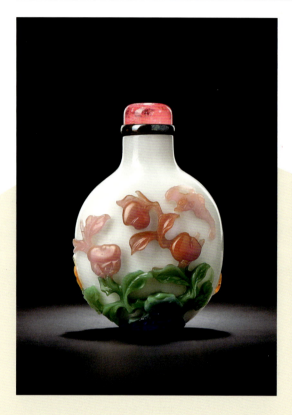
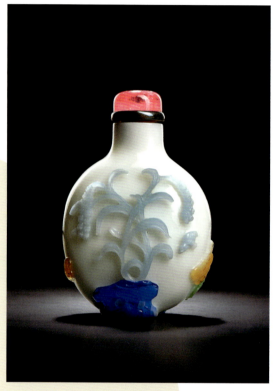

66

清 白地套多色玻璃「歲歲平安」鼻煙壺

玻璃鼻煙壺，呈扁瓶形。直口，溜肩，腹下漸收，平底。通體涅白地套粉紅、水藍、綠、黃、藍等五色玻璃。以多色顯花，腹壁兩面皆以剔地技法，高浮雕吉祥紋樣。一面套粉紅、綠色料雕飾桃樹蝙蝠，寓意「福壽雙全」；另一面套水藍、黃色料雕飾稻穗與鵪鶉，表徵「歲歲平安」。近底足兩側與底部，則以藍料雕飾崖石海濤，隱喻「壽山福海」之意。全器用色鮮活，層次清新且紋樣清雅高潔，能臻上品珍玩之流。

1750-1820年
高：5.2 厘米

A glass bottle, of rounded form, with a cylindrical neck and a wide mouth; overlaid with six colors – pink, rose-pink, green, yellow, cobalt-blue and pale blue – on a milk-white ground; one main side carved with a bat flying above flowering leafy plants, including a peach tree, issuing from rockwork; the reverse carved with sprays of millet issuing from rockwork with a small quail to one side.

Attributed to Beijing

1750-1820
Height: 5.2 cm

67

清　珍珠地套九色玻璃花卉草蟲鼻煙壺

玻璃鼻煙壺，呈扁瓶形。直口，溜肩，深腹，腹下漸收，橢圓形圈足。通體無色透明珍珠地套紅、綠、深藍、琥珀、粉紅、淺綠、海藍、綠松、孔雀藍等九色玻璃，以多色顯花，於腹壁雕飾各色折枝牡丹、靈芝仙草、蝴蝶等花卉草蟲，多彩圖像既象徵春色，也寓意富貴長壽。

是件鼻煙壺用色多彩繽紛，依類賦彩，形象鮮明。特別是九色玻璃的完美搭配，正代表套色玻璃技術邁向登峰造極的最高境界。

1750-1850年
高：6.4 厘米

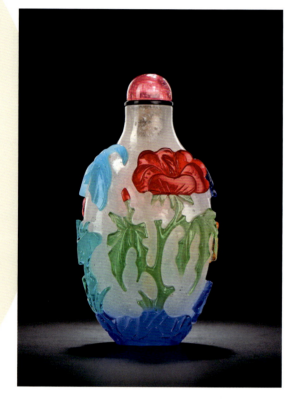

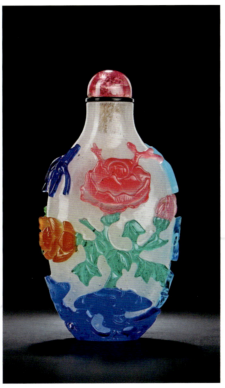

A glass bottle, of flattened, ovoid form, with a cylindrical neck and a wide mouth; overlaid with nine colors – translucent red, rose-pink, green, teal, cobalt-blue, sky-blue, aquamarine, amber and turquoise – on a snowflake ground; one main side carved with leafy flowering peonies, issuing from rockwork with a butterfly flitting above; the reverse carved with a mallow flower issuing from rockwork; one narrow side carved with *lingzhi* and grasses.

Attributed to Beijing

1750-1850
Height: 6.4 cm

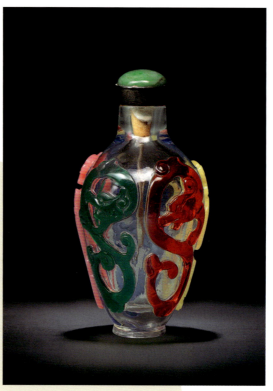

68

清　透明地套五色玻璃蟠螭紋鼻煙壺

玻璃鼻煙壺，作罐形。直口，溜肩，腹下斜削至底部，圈足。
通體白色透明地套藍、紅、綠、黃、粉紅等五色玻璃，於腹
壁貼飾呈環繞排列狀的淺浮雕五色蟠螭，蟠螭昂首直立，身
軀做S形屈曲，長尾上翹。整體形象鮮活，線條轉折流暢，
在透明玻璃的映襯下，五種不同顏色的蟠螭，別有一番視覺
饗宴。

1750-1850年
高：6.2 厘米

A glass bottle, of *meiping* form, with shoulders sloping to a cylindrical neck and with a neatly carved circular footrim; overlaid with five colors – blue, pink, green, red and yellow – on a transparent ground, continuously carved with five coiling *chilong* running vertically from the shoulders to the foot.

Attributed to Beijing

1750-1850
Height: 6.2 cm

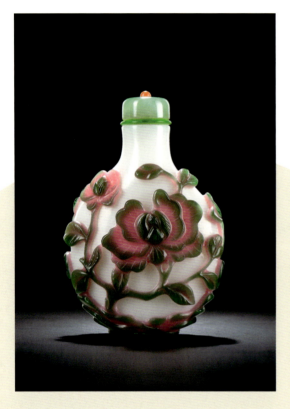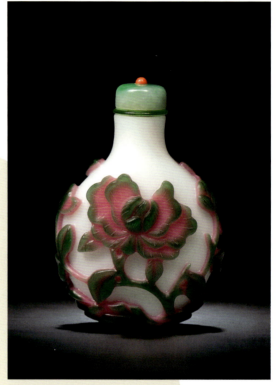

69

清　白地疊套紅綠色玻璃牡丹紋鼻煙壺

玻璃鼻煙壺，呈扁瓶形。直口，溜肩，腹下漸收，橢圓形圈
足。通體涅白地套粉紅、淡綠二色玻璃，腹壁兩面以疊套技
法，浮雕湖石牡丹紋，牡丹朵花以粉紅色顯花，花蕊周緣疊壓
綠色滾邊，剛好與枝葉的綠色顯花相互輝映。全器素雅高潔，
花開富貴，秀美可人。

1750-1820年
高：5.7 厘米

A glass bottle, of flattened, rounded form with shoulders tapering to a cylindrical neck, and with a neatly carved oval footrim; overlaid in olive-green on pink on a milk-white ground; carved on each main side with flowering leafy peonies issuing from rockwork.

Attributed to Beijing

1750-1820
Height: 5.7 cm

70

清　白地疊套紅綠色玻璃提籃海棠鼻煙壺

玻璃鼻煙壺，呈扁瓶形。直口，溜肩，腹下漸收，橢圓形圈足。通體涅白地疊套粉紅、碧綠二色玻璃，腹部下方近底足處，淺浮雕以碧綠色顯花的提籃，提籃編織紋刻劃精細，提樑向右平置，籃內裝扁瓶，瓶腹上二色顯花，為折枝海棠花。全器造型獨特，設計新穎，讓人意味無窮。

1780-1850年
高：7.1 厘米

A glass bottle, of rounded form with shoulders tapering to a cylindrical neck, and with a neatly carved oval footrim; overlaid in green on pink on a milk-white ground; carved on each main side with a wicker basket full of blossoming flowers, its handle resting to one side.

Attributed to Beijing

1780-1850
Height: 7.1 cm

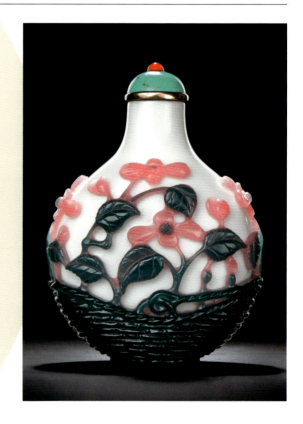

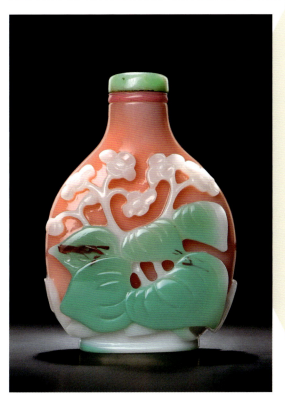

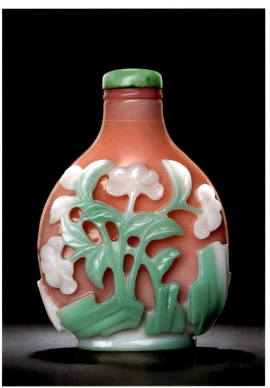

清　粉紅地疊套粉綠白色玻璃湖石花卉鼻煙壺

玻璃鼻煙壺，呈扁瓶形。直口，溜肩，腹下漸收，橢圓形圈足。通體粉紅地疊套粉綠、白二色玻璃，腹壁兩面雕工，一面浮雕折枝海棠，另一面浮雕湖石牡丹，表徵「玉堂富貴」之意。所飾圖樣，朵花以白色顯花，枝葉與湖石則以綠色表現。全器湖石花卉宛如書畫上的沒骨畫法，大筆揮就，酣暢淋漓，具恣意灑脫的藝術氣韻。

1780-1850年
高：6.7 厘米

A glass bottle, of flattened, rounded form with shoulders tapering to a cylindrical neck, and with a neatly carved oval footrim; overlaid in pale-green on white on an opaque pink ground; carved on each main side with leafy flowering plants issuing from rockwork.

Attributed to Beijing

1780-1850
Height: 6.7 cm

清　白地疊套紅白玻璃雙龍競逐紋鼻煙壺

玻璃鼻煙壺，呈扁瓶形。直口，溜肩，腹下漸收，橢圓形圈
足。通體涅白地疊套紅、白兩色玻璃，腹壁兩面以疊套技法，
浮雕花下壓花式的雙龍競逐。全器先用紅色玻璃於頸部飾蕉葉
紋，腹部飾雲紋錦地，然後復以白色玻璃於紅色玻璃紋樣上，
飾海濤紋與雙龍競逐紋。雙龍作五爪，形象威猛，在紅、白兩
色玻璃的熔融下，略呈紫色，別有一番風韻。底署「怡水」二
字篆書款。

1750-1820年
高：6.6 厘米

A glass bottle, of rounded form with shoulders tapering
to a cylindrical neck, and with a neatly carved oval
footrim; overlaid in white on ruby-red on a snowflake
ground; continuously carved with a coiling scaly dragon
flying through scrolling clouds in pursuit of a flaming
pearl, a second dragon rising from frothy waves below;
the neck with a band of overlapping Artemis leaves,
the base with a two-character mark "Yi Shui" (Pleasant
Water) overlaid in red.

Attributed to Beijing

1750-1820
Height: 6.6 cm

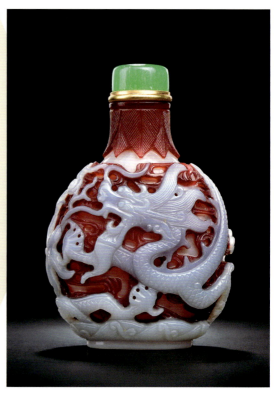

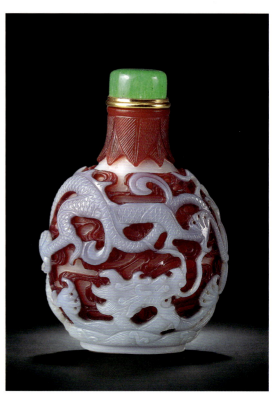

73

清　丁二仲款玻璃內繪山水亭閣鼻煙壺

玻璃鼻煙壺，呈扁瓶形。直口，溜肩，深腹，橢圓形圈足。腹壁兩面以內繪技術，一面繪通景式的山水亭閣，並署「孟延仁兄大人正，庚寫」另一面以各類書體署，書：「登明選公，雜進巧拙。紆餘為妍，卓犖為傑。」金文：「重作陣尊」，楷書：「顧愷之每食蔗，必自尾至本，或問其故，曰：漸入佳境。」篆書：「壽如金石，佳且好兮，長宜子孫。」並摹繪「元康二年作」瓦當殘影，末署「二仲」款。

丁二仲（1868-1935年），原名丁尚庚，亦作上庚，藝作均署二仲，遂以此行。浙江紹興人，幼隨父於河北通州任所定居。丁氏不但對內繪藝術精通，而且對金石、篆刻、竹刻頗有研究，是晚清著名的藝術家。其山水、人物、花鳥俱擅，畫風博雅深邃，別具一格。與周樂元、馬少宣、葉仲三等，號稱晚清內繪四大家。

約1894年
高：5.7厘米

右：
「登明選公，雜進巧拙。紆餘為妍，卓犖為傑。」

左上（金文）：
「重作陣尊」，「顧愷之每食蔗，必自尾至本，或問其故，曰：漸入佳境。」

左下：
「壽如金石，佳且好兮，長宜子孫。」

正下：
「元康二年作」「二仲」

另一面署：
「孟延仁兄大人正，庚寫。」

A glass bottle, of flattened, rectangular form with a cylindrical neck and a neatly carved oval footrim, painted on the inside using ink and watercolors, one main side with a mountainous landscape with a river running between massive rockwork with pavilions nestled in the trees along both sides of the river, a figure looking out at the water from one of the pavilions, beneath an inscription reading: "Respectfully presented to benevolent older-brother Mr. Meng Yanren, painted by Yu."

The reverse with lines of calligraphy in different scripts above fragments of two archaic bronze rubbings, the inscriptions reading:

Right: "Select the talents with transparency and fairness, so that both the intellect and those less smart are promoted, restraint is regarded with grace, while excellence is extraordinary."

Upper left: (taken from an inscription on a bronze) "Reproducing the Zhen *zun* [bronze ritual vessel]."

Middle left: "Whenever Gu Kaizhi ate the sugarcane, he always started from the root upwards. When someone asked him why, he replied, to reach the blissful realm gradually."

Lower left: "Long life is like bronze and stone, beautiful and good, an everlasting blessing for the offspring."

The rubbings towards the base reading: "Made in the second year of Yuankang", and signed 'Erzhong' with one red seal.

Attributed to Beijing

Circa 1894
Height: 5.7 cm

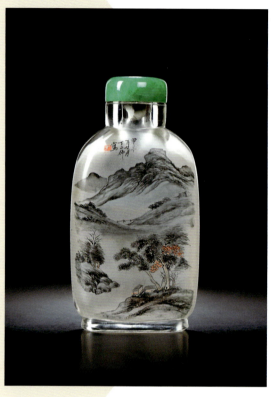

74

清　丁二仲款玻璃內繪山水圖鼻煙壺

玻璃鼻煙壺，呈扁瓶形。直口，溜肩，深腹，橢圓形圈足。腹壁兩面以內繪技術畫山水圖，一面高樹矗立湖畔，亭閣掩映林間，對岸屋宇數幢，遠岫遙岑，墨色清淡，頗富層次。畫面上方留白處署「仿黃鶴山樵，孟延仁兄大人雅屬」。末署「丁二仲」。另一面所繪山水構圖雷同，惟於中景布局略作變化，亦於畫面上方署「甲午夏月，丁二仲寫。」

考鼻煙壺所署甲午年款，根據丁二仲的生卒年推斷，應指1894年。又所題「仿黃鶴山樵」者，當指元代畫家王蒙。有關丁二仲生平，可參閱本書作品編號73。

1894年
高：6.2厘米

一面上方留白處署：
「仿黃鶴山樵，孟延仁兄大人雅屬。」
末署：
「丁二仲」

另一面署：
「甲午夏月，丁二仲寫。」

A glass bottle, of flattened, rectangular form with a cylindrical neck and a neatly carved oval footrim, painted on the inside using ink and watercolors, each main side with a mountainous landscape with a river running between massive rockwork with pavilions nestled in the trees along both sides of the river; one side with an inscription reading:

"In imitation of the wood-cutter of Yellow Crane Mountain, at the elegant request of respected benevolent older-brother Meng Yanren," and signed 'Ding Erzhong'

the reverse with "Executed by Ding Erzhong in the summer month of Jiawu year (1894)"

with one red seal.

Attributed to Beijing

1894
Height: 6.2 cm

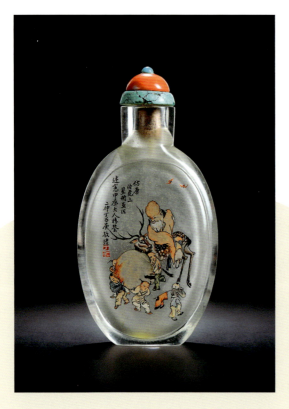

75

清　丁二仲款玻璃內繪福祿壽三星圖鼻煙壺

玻璃鼻煙壺，呈扁瓶形。直口，溜肩，弧腹，橢圓形圈足。腹壁兩面以內繪技術，一面繪壽翁騎鹿，童子捧桃圖，表徵福祿壽的吉祥寓意。並於畫面左上方署：「仿唐伯虎三星冊畫法。述憲中丞大人雅鑒，二仲丁尚庚，敬遺。」並鈐「丁」、「二中」二方款。另一面則畫剪影式的書畫、碑文與瓦當拓本。亦於左上方署：「乙巳夏五月，二仲‧庚，繪於十七樓梅花山館。」末鈐「二中」二字印章款。

考鼻煙壺所署乙巳年款，根據丁二仲的生卒年推斷，應指1905年。有關丁二仲生平，可參閱本書作品編號73。

1905年
高：6.4 厘米

左上方署：
「仿唐伯虎三星冊畫法。述憲中丞大人雅鑒，

二仲丁尚庚，敬遺。」

並鈐二方款：

「丁」、「二中」

另一面：

「乙巳夏五月，二仲，庚，

繪於十七樓梅花山館。」

末鈐二字印章款：

「二中」

A glass bottle, of flattened, ovoid form with a cylindrical neck and a flat oval foot, painted on the inside using ink and watercolors within an ovoid panel, one main side with a scene of Shoulao on a spotted deer looking back at a group of young boys carrying a large ripe peach with two bats flying above him below an inscription reading: "Painted in imitation of Tang Bohu's Three Star Album, made for the elegant appraisal of His Excellency, the governor, executed and respectfully presented by Ding Erzhong," and signed Ding Erzhong with two red seals, 'Ding,' and 'Erzhong'; the reverse with fragments of archaic bronze rubbings and a painting of a pine tree, signed: "Painted by Erzhong Yu in the fifth summer month, *Yishi* year (1905), at the Mouqiang Hill Study in the seventeenth tower," followed by the seal 'Erzhong'.

Attributed to Beijing

1905
Height: 6.4 cm

76

民國　涅白胎玻璃畫琺瑯花卉—虞美人鼻煙壺

玻璃鼻煙壺，呈罐形。敞口，短束頸，豐肩，腹下漸收至底足急斂，圈足。通體不透明玻璃胎上繪琺瑯彩，口緣下方飾一匝藍彩弦紋，弦紋下繪多彩變形蕉葉如意雲肩勾連雲紋一圈，腹壁繪通景式洞石虞美人花卉，洞石表現出陰陽向背，花葉先以細筆勾形，然後隨類賦彩，設色鮮麗柔美，筆觸細膩，具工筆畫韻致。底署藍彩「乾隆年製」四字楷書款。

虞美人又名蝴蝶滿春，屬罌粟科罌粟屬草本植物，花期夏季，花色有紅、白、紫、藍等顏色，濃艷華美。

1933-1943年
高：5.4 厘米

An enamel on glass bottle, of *meiping* form with a cylindrical neck with slightly everted mouth, and with a neatly carved circular footrim; decorated using *famille-rose* enamels on milk-white glass with a continuous scene of leafy flowering shrubs, including peonies, poppies and daisies, and grasses growing on a grassy bank beside convoluted rockwork; the neck with a band of Artemis leaves between an interlocking scrolling border and a border of *lingzhi* heads; the base with a blue enamel four-character *Qianlong nian zhi* mark in regular script.

Attributed to Ye Bengqi, Beijing.

1933-1943
Height: 5.4 cm

蘇州流派（蘇作）

當我們提到蘇州流派，相比於其他亞洲藝術品，鼻煙壺的劃分更加明確具體，但這種劃分不一定精準。1787年後，蘇州齊集了大量工匠，在乾隆皇帝的影響下，開始雕刻畫片精美的玉山子和玉屏。

蘇州流派的玉鼻煙壺與瑪瑙鼻煙壺辨析度高，常指帶有以下明顯特徵的作品：

- 題材多為寫實的自然景物而非宮廷的圖案化紋飾；
- 利用石頭自身的紋理和顏色凸顯紋樣；
- 帶虛假的落款以及題詩；
- 工匠可以實現多層次雕刻；
- 將寶石的雕刻技術運用到玉髓和水晶等各式材質。

蘇州流派所製器物，如鼻煙壺，可以通過這些明顯的特徵辨認出來，形成一個特殊的門類。可是，以上這些特徵並不是一個一成不變的單子，更像是一套通用守則。更重要的是整體概念，工匠腦海中的想法是他們製作鼻煙壺以及其他工藝品的基礎，超越世俗，將他們從日常生活的約束中解放出來。這體現在工匠們利用石材本身，包括其內含雜質設計出立體的雕塑效果，他們運用不同的工藝實現這種效果，比如，多層雕刻以及減地雕刻，這使得作品更具立體感與透視感。蘇州流派所製玉鼻煙壺與瑪瑙鼻煙壺，二者器形驚人一致，多作圓形和橢圓形，無圈足，最大限度地利用壺身空間進行裝飾，器形簡潔，以突出精湛的雕刻工藝。蘇作作品，器形對稱規整，壺身圓形開光，讓工匠們得以自由地發揮其精湛的技藝、根據石材設計紋飾、不受外在器形的限制。工匠根據石材本身的特徵與內含物，而非器物的形狀，來決定是做正反兩面設計還是做通景設計。

蘇州流派其中的一個特徵是湖石。雖然並不是每一個蘇作鼻煙壺均雕刻湖石，但大部分都有。蘇州以庭院聞名，至今仍擁有大量觀賞奇石，因此蘇作鼻煙壺上雕湖石便順理成章。蘇作鼻煙壺所刻之湖石可分為三類：或邊緣呈鋸齒狀、或邊緣圓潤、或多層疊加而成，三者相互搭配。

怪石嶙峋、煙雲迷漫，人物如高士、賢者、漁人立於其間，工匠巧借石材的天然色差表現人物衣袍、帽子及配飾。常見的動物題材有馬上封侯、飛禽、海魚等，另有劉海戲金蟾等神話人物，卻不見龍紋，可知其重要性。我們無法全面了解其成因，龍是中國傳統文化的固有組成部分，除了在迫切情況下需要描繪龍作為帝王象徵，龍不會出現在非宮廷器物之上。蘇作玉器另一個典型的畫片特徵是常用子料的玉皮去突出設計與雕工。

蘇作利用玉色強化效果。有一組稀有但工藝絕倫的黑、灰、白玉巧雕鼻煙壺，雕黑玉為地，白玉與淺灰玉作紋飾。一般背景以淺浮雕或暗刻工藝裝飾，增加整体細節。有的作品雙面皆雕刻畫片；有的作品背面暗刻詩文，個別帶落款。很多藏家視這類黑白玉巧雕鼻煙壺為蘇州流派的精品，因其完美地把審美與工藝相結合，這是其他地方作坊無法達到的。

題詩也是蘇州流派作品的特別之處，它常以不同的形式在鼻煙壺壺身不同的地方出現。一些黑、灰、白玉鼻煙壺，常刻詩詞於壺身，多在背面；瑪瑙鼻煙壺，常刻於湖石上或者畫片空白處。

SUZHOU SCHOOL

The snuff bottle world is rather more specific than in the rest of the Asian art world when it refers to the Suzhou School of carving, although it is not necessarily more accurate. After 1787 many carvers in Suzhou, under the influence of the Qianlong Emperor, began carving jade mountains or panels in what the emperor called a 'pictorial mood'.

Concerning snuff bottles in both jade and agate, this label refers to a recognizable group that shares the following predominant features:

- The portrayal of naturalistic subject matter that is less formalized than 'imperial' subject matter.
- The use of the natural fissures and colors in the stone to highlight the design.
- The occurrence of spurious signatures and poetic inscriptions.
- The ability of the carver to work through several planes of stone.
- The translation of lapidary techniques over to different materials such as chalcedony and crystal.

Objects, including snuff bottles from the Suzhou School, are recognized by these specific characteristics which together form a unified group. However, this is not a fixed list, but a more general set of rules. It is the overall concept that is more important and which in the minds of the carvers have allowed them to produce bottles, and other works of art, which transcend the mundane by freeing them from the constraints of their everyday activities. This concept is realized through the design where every part of the stone including its natural inclusions is used by the carver producing a three-dimensional sculptural effect. This is achieved in several ways, for example, by using the different planes of carving and undercutting which produce works that are sculptural and with perspective. The shape of bottles from the Suzhou School in both jade and agate is strikingly consistent. Generally, of a rounded or ovoid form with no footrim, they allow the maximum amount of space for the design with the simple outline allowing no distractions from the more elaborate carving. The importance of form to the Suzhou School with its symmetrical regularity and plain rounded sides is that it gives the carver the freedom to develop his skills and execute the design indicated by the material without being hampered by the outer frame of the object. Even the choice of whether to have two differently carved sides or a continuous scene around the bottle is not dictated by its shape but by the markings or inclusions in the stone itself.

One of the classic features of the Suzhou School is rockwork. Whilst it is not a hard and fast rule that a 'Suzhou School' bottle needs to have a rock of some form on it, many bottles do exhibit this characteristic. It is hardly surprising as Suzhou, often referred to as the 'City of Gardens' has more than its fair share of ornamental rocks, even today. Rockwork on bottles of the Suzhou School appear to fall into three types, often used in combination with each other - these are referred to as 'serrated' rockwork, 'convoluted' rockwork, and 'multiple-plane' rockwork.

Amidst the dramatic rockwork and beneath the scrolling clouds are figures; scholars, sages, and fishermen - their clothes, hats, and other accouterments highlighted by the carver's skillful use of the stone's natural coloring. Often animals such as monkeys and horses are portrayed, birds of the air and fish of the sea are common subject matters. And whilst mythical figures such as Liu hai and his three-legged toad are depicted, dragons tend to be significant by their absence. The reasoning for this is not entirely clear as dragons were an inherent part of Chinese culture except that the urgency to portray the emperor, symbolically or otherwise, would be lacking on pieces that were not bound for the palace. In jade, one classic characteristic of the 'pictorial' mood of the Suzhou School is the use of the outer russet skin of the jade riverbed pebbles to highlight the design or carving.

The Suzhou School uses color with dramatic effect. There is a small superbly made group of black, grey, and white jade bottles where the white or pale grey inclusions are carved against the black ground. Often the ground itself is also carved in lower relief or incised to add more detail to the subject. In some cases, both sides have been carved pictorially, in other cases the reverse side has been incised with a poetic inscription and is accompanied occasionally by a signature. The 'black and white' jade bottles are, to many collectors, the zenith of this school combining artistry and technique to a degree that is lacking elsewhere.

The Suzhou School is also renowned for its inscriptions appearing in various guises and locations on the bottles. On a number of the black, gray, and white nephrite group the inscription is incised on one face of the bottle, usually accepted as the reverse of the piece, whilst on agate bottles, it is often carved into the smooth face of the rockwork or to one side of the scene.

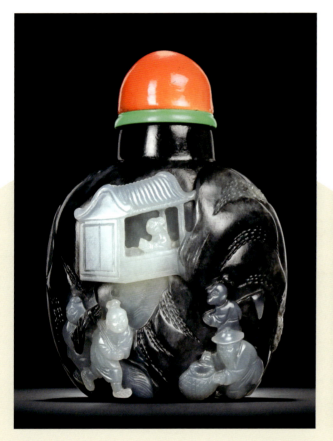

77

清　黑白玉巧雕「漁樵耕讀」蘇作鼻煙壺

鼻煙壺整料和闐玉雕成，玉色黑白交融。呈扁瓶形。直口，豐肩，弧腹，腹下近底足漸收，臥足。正面利用白玉質地，突出人物與屋宇的刻畫，屋宇依陡峭山勢而建，其下流水潺潺，屋內一人正展書課讀。屋外三四人，或立或蹲，分別作負薪、耕田、乃至捕魚的表徵性動作，呈現一派農忙的和樂景象。另一面以壓地隱起技法，淺浮雕松壑巨崖，並於崖壁留白處題辭，字跡錯落，不易辨識。末署：乙卯仲秋，平江。並鐫鈐「国」字款。

是件鼻煙壺造型渾圓飽滿，俏色分明，雕工精細，是一件頗具文人意趣的蘇作鼻煙壺。

年份：1795或1855年
高：7.4 厘米

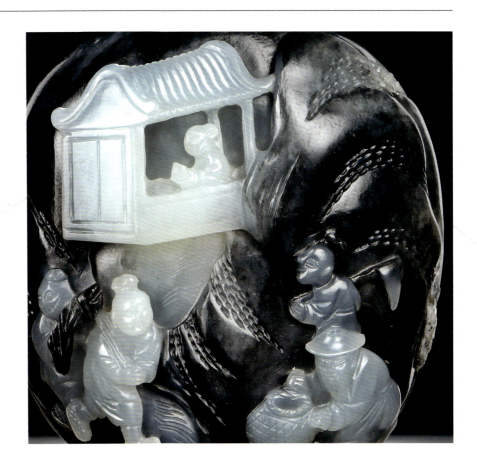

A nephrite bottle, of black, gray and white tones, well hollowed, of ovoid form with a cylindrical neck and a concave oval foot; carved on one main side in relief using the paler colors as a cameo with a scene of a figure reading a book in a pavilion in a rocky landscape and observing a wood-cutter, a farmer and a fisherman outside; the other side carved with trees overhanging serrated rockwork on which are engraved a series of long inscriptions and a date.

Attributed to Suzhou

Date: 1795 or 1855
Height: 7.4 cm

78

清　黃玉巧雕「李白醉酒」蘇作鼻煙壺

鼻煙壺整料和闐玉雕成，玉色淡黃，局部有白、黑色共生
玉質。通體作扁瓶形。直口，豐肩，弧腹，腹下近底足漸
收，圈足。腹壁一面利用不同玉色巧雕李白醉酒圖，但見
李白倚坐壘石上，一旁童僕正舉壺斟酒，形像刻畫李白飲
酒賦詩的情狀。另一面則以壓地隱起技法，淺浮雕杜甫詩
句：「天子呼來不上船，自稱臣是酒中仙。」書用行草，
短短十四字一氣呵成，如行雲流水，疏逸雅致。

1780-1880年
高：6.3 厘米

一面浮雕：
「天子呼來不上船，
自稱臣是酒中仙。」

A nephrite bottle, of black, gray and white tones, well hollowed, of ovoid form with a cylindrical neck and a concave oval foot; carved on one main side in relief using the darker colors as a cameo with a mountainous landscape scene of the poet, Li Bai seated on a rock, having wine poured for him by his attendant; the other side carved in raised relief with a lengthy inscription reading:

"When summoned by the Son of Heaven, Li Bai refused to board the boat, declaring,
I, your subject, am an immortal of the wine-cup."

Attributed to Suzhou

1780-1880
Height: 6.3 cm

79

清　白玉帶皮巧雕「輩輩封侯」蘇作鼻煙壺

鼻煙壺整料和闐玉雕成，局部帶褐色皮，屬蘇作工。通體作扁瓶形。直口，溜肩，垂腹，腹下近底足漸收，平底。腹壁一面以剔地技法，浮雕屈曲的老松，岩塊間靈芝迸生，並利用皮色巧雕五隻靈猴相互疊背攀坐於老松上，樹梢蜂窩旁有隻蜜蜂，有「輩輩封侯」的寓意。

另一面任光素，刻意展現褐色玉皮的渾然天成。

1780-1850年
高：6.3 厘米

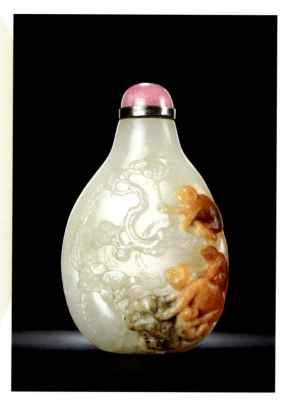

A nephrite bottle, of white tone with honey-brown and dark brown inclusions, well hollowed, of teardrop shape with a cylindrical neck and a concave oval foot; carved on one main side in relief using the darker colors as a cameo with a mountainous landscape scene of a group of monkeys clambering on rocks and in a pine tree; the other side with the russet skin of the pebble left uncarved.

Attributed to Suzhou

1780-1850
Height: 6.3 cm

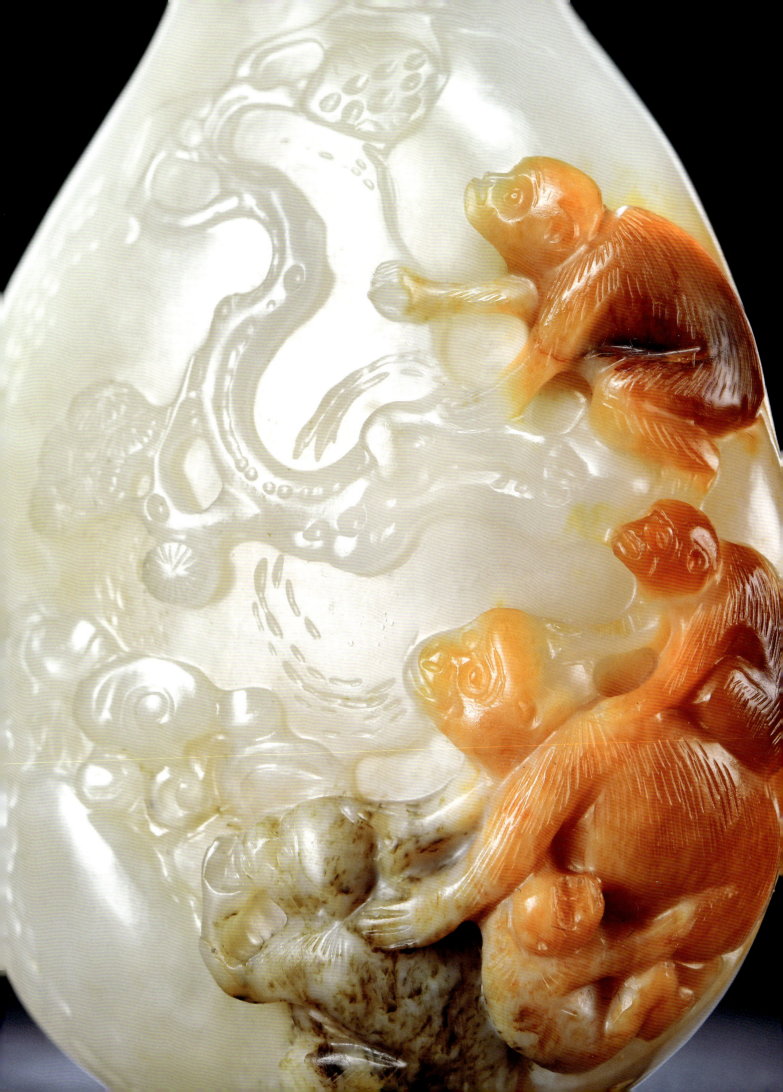

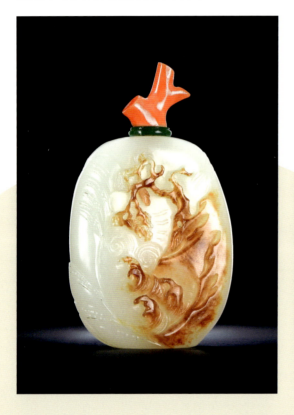

80

清　白玉帶皮巧雕「壽山福海」蘇作鼻煙壺

鼻煙壺整料和闐玉雕成，局部帶褐色皮，屬蘇作工。通體略呈
扁平卵石狀，底部削切做橢圓形圈足。兩面雕工，一面淺浮雕
巨石岩縫間有靈芝迸生。另一面利用大面積褐色皮，飾危崖孤
松下，海濤洶湧，代表「壽山福海」的吉祥象徵。壽山福海題
材，似乎來自明朝典故，因宰相劉基嘗有歌曰：「壽比南山，
福如東海。」因此後世便以「壽山福海」形容福氣像東海一樣
浩大，壽命如終南山一般長久般的人間美事。

1780-1850年
高：5.7 厘米

A nephrite bottle, of white tone with honey-brown inclusions, well hollowed, of pebble form with a concave oval foot; carved on one main side in relief using the darker colors as a cameo with a mountainous landscape scene of trees and shrubs growing amongst craggy serrated rocks; the reverse with a similar scene.

Attributed to Suzhou

1780-1850
Height: 5.7 cm

81

清　白玉巧雕雙獾及仙人放鶴蘇作鼻煙壺

鼻煙壺整料和闐玉雕成，局部帶礓皮，屬蘇作工。通體作扁瓶
形。直口，溜肩，弧腹，腹下近底足漸收，平底。腹壁兩面雕
工，一面以淺浮雕技法飾一老翁坐於巨崖斜樹下，高舉右臂，
指向於空中飛翔的仙鶴，表徵長壽之意。另一面則以高浮雕技
法，利用礓皮巧雕松下雙獾。全器雕工精細，刻劃鮮活，尤其
是利用礓皮巧雕的藝術手法，更有化腐朽為神奇的匠心獨運。

1780-1880年
高：6.1厘米

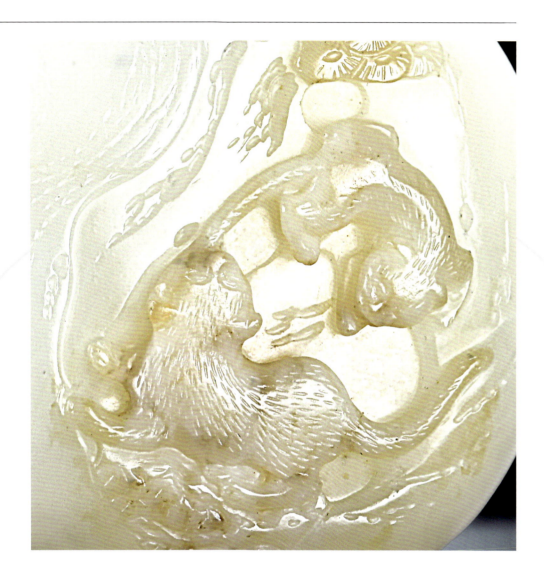

A nephrite bottle, of white tone with brown inclusions, well hollowed, of ovoid form with a cylindrical neck and a concave oval foot; carved on one main side in relief using the darker colors as a cameo with the Daoist fable of a scholar seated leaning against a rock under a gnarly pine tree, his staff by his side, looking up at a crane in flight, released by him; the reverse with two badgers playing beside a massive serrated rocky outcrop from which a pine tree grows.

Attributed to Suzhou

1780-1880
Height: 6.1 cm

82

清　白玉雕「米顛拜石」蘇作鼻煙壺

鼻煙壺整料和闐玉雕成，玉質潔白，姣好凝潤。通體作扁瓶
形。直口，豐肩，弧腹，腹下漸收，平底。腹壁以浮雕技法，
一面雕米顛拜石；一面雕李白醉酒圖。兩圖皆作通景式構圖，
米芾面對庭園洞石，兀自拱手行禮，表現愛石的獨特癖好，
故稱米顛拜石。而李白在湖石蕉蔭下，緊貼酒罈豪飲的意象，
正是李白醉酒的典型畫面。

1780-1850年
高：5.4 厘米

A nephrite bottle, of even white tone, well hollowed, of rounded form with a cylindrical neck and a concave oval foot; carved on one main side in relief with a mountainous landscape scene of the poet, Li Bai seated beside a massive rock under a pine tree with a large wine jar beside him, his attendant to the rear; the reverse with Mi Fu bowing to a massive rock under a pine tree, with his attendant kneeling behind him; the shoulders with a mantle of scrolling clouds.

Attributed to Suzhou

1780-1850
Height: 5.4 cm

83

清　瑪瑙巧雕「英雄得利」蘇作鼻煙壺

鼻煙壺整料天然瑪瑙雕成，呈扁瓶形。直口，溜肩，弧腹，腹下漸收，平底。通體於腹壁兩面利用瑪瑙的俏色巧雕，一面浮雕兩漁樵於汀渚岸邊垂釣，另一面則蒼鷹停佇松塈，巨熊緩行水湄，表徵「英雄得利」之意。一旁留白處並署「得利圖」三字。

1780-1850年
高：5.9 厘米

An agate bottle, very well hollowed, of rounded bulbous
form with a cylindrical neck and a flat oval foot, of
honey-brown and dark brown tones, carved on one main
side in relief using the darker colors as a cameo with a
scene of two fishermen seated on rocks beside a river
beside pine trees, one with a fishing basket at his side
and casting his rod into the water, the other standing on
a large fish on the bank; the reverse with an eagle and
a smaller bird perched in a pine tree which grows from
a rock, a white bear below them, observing a fisherman
standing on a rock, pulling a fish out of the waves below,
a three-character inscription in raised relief reading:
"Picture of attaining success"; the shoulders with a
mantle of scrolling clouds.

Attributed to Suzhou

1780-1850
Height: 5.9 cm

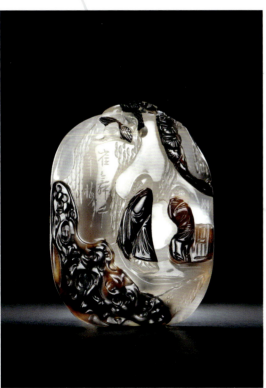

附：清　瑪瑙巧雕蘇作橢圓牌

蘇作瑪瑙牌呈橢圓形，亦利用瑪瑙的天然俏色巧雕。一面雕一著袍衣的仙翁，立於蒼松下仰望凌空舞鶴，留白處署「鶴舞千年樹」。另一面飾一長髯老翁端坐蒲席，似在面壁修行，一旁亦署有「仙家歲月長」。全器雕工渾圓，顏色對比鮮明，展現蘇作工藝的精湛造詣。

1780-1850年
高：6 厘米

An agate pendant, of flattened oval shape, of pale gray, honey-brown and dark brown tones, carved on one main side in relief using the darker colors as a cameo with a scene of Mi Fu reading the inscription, "Cranes dance above the ancient trees" on a massive rock under a pine tree, with his attendant kneeling behind him, a crane in flight on the upper left corner; the reverse with a similar scene of a scholar seated under a pine tree, before a massive rock on which is written an inscription, "The years are long in the house of the Immortal", his attendant nearby standing between two rocks.

Attributed to Suzhou

1780-1850
Height: 6 cm

84

清　瑪瑙巧雕「三元(猿)圖」蘇作鼻煙壺

鼻煙壺整料天然瑪瑙雕成，呈扁瓶形。直口，溜肩，弧腹，
腹下漸收，橢圓形圈足。屬蘇作工，腹壁兩面皆利用瑪瑙的
俏色巧雕，作通景式構圖，首先利用褐色質地巧雕巨石岩洞，
岩洞縫隙有靈芝迸出，岩洞內有三隻靈猴蹲坐，身體姿態略
有不同，分別作遮眼、眼耳、搗嘴的動作，表徵非禮勿視、
非禮勿聽以及非禮勿言的意思。並於畫面較疏朗的留白處，
署「三元圖」三字。

1780-1850年
高：5.5 厘米

An agate bottle, very well hollowed, of rounded bulbous form with a cylindrical neck and with a neatly carved oval footrim, of honey-brown and dark brown tones, carved on one main side in relief using the darker colors as a cameo with a scene of three monkeys seated on rocky outcrops, one eating a peach, surrounded by scrolling clouds, with *lingzhi* growing to one side; the reverse with a peach tree burgeoned with ripe peaches beside an inscription reading: "Picture of success in the imperial examinations thrice over"; the shoulders with a mantle of scrolling clouds.

Attributed to Suzhou

1780-1850
Height: 5.5 cm

85

清　瑪瑙巧雕「李白醉酒」蘇作鼻煙壺

鼻煙壺整料天然瑪瑙雕成，呈扁瓶形。直口，溜肩，弧腹，腹
下漸收，平底。腹壁兩面作通景式構圖，屬蘇作工，利用瑪瑙
的天然俏色巧雕。深褐色部分用以勾勒衣服、花葉、洞石與酒
罈，淺褐色的大部分肌理則以陰刻技法勾劃庭園圍欄與人物面
容，於是一幅大家耳熟能詳的李白醉酒圖也就躍然紙上了。

1780-1850年
高：4.8 厘米

An agate bottle, very well hollowed; of rounded bulbous
form with a cylindrical neck and a slightly everted
mouth, and a flat oval foot, of honey-brown and dark
brown tones; carved on one main side in relief using
the darker colors as a cameo with a scene of the poet, Li
Bai seated beside a massive rock under a pine tree with
a wine jar beside him; the reverse with a mountainous
landscape with massive rockwork; the shoulders with a
mantle of scrolling clouds.

Attributed to Suzhou

1780-1850
Height: 4.8 cm

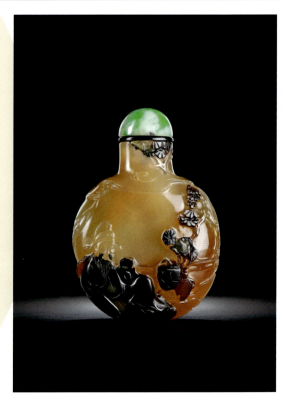

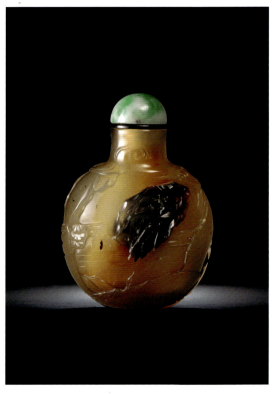

附：清　瑪瑙巧雕蘇作長方牌

瑪瑙牌呈委角長方形，利用天然俏色巧雕，屬蘇作工。一面以浮雕技法，巧雕米顛拜石圖，另一面則以壓地隱起技法，淺浮雕「真堅誰似石，禮拜豈云癡」十字詩句。全器人物刻畫鮮明，構圖突出，所鐫字體跌宕灑脫，能於靈動中見骨氣，可謂圖文並茂也。

1780-1850年
高：4.5 厘米

An agate pendant, of flattened rectangular shape with rounded corners, of pale gray, honey-brown and dark brown tones; carved on one main side in relief using the darker colors as a cameo with a scene of Mi Fu bowing to a massive rock under a pine tree, with his attendant fanning him from behind; the reverse carved in raised relief with a ten-character inscription reading: "Connected so deeply to the stone, who would say [Mi Fu] is senseless to worship it," with a border of craggy rocks.

Attributed to Suzhou

1780-1850
Height: 4.5 cm

一面雕：
「真堅誰似石，禮拜豈云癡。」

86

清　瑪瑙巧雕「松壑立馬」蘇作鼻煙壺

鼻煙壺整料天然瑪瑙雕成，呈扁瓶形。直口，溜肩，弧腹，腹下漸收，平底。屬蘇作工，兩面利用俏色巧雕。一面淺浮雕巨岩緩坡處有一回首立馬，立馬嘴套絡頭，一旁童子手拉韁繩，似在等候主人的歸來。另一面摹刻松壑靈芝，表現杳無人跡的深山景象，留白處署「仙翁道德深」五字。

1780-1850年
高：5.6 厘米

An agate bottle, very well hollowed; of rounded bulbous form with a cylindrical neck and a slightly everted mouth, and a flat oval foot, of grayish-brown and dark brown tones; carved on one main side in relief using the darker colors as a cameo with a mountainous landscape scene of craggy rockwork and pine trees, with a figure pulling a horse from the river; the reverse with massive serrated rockwork from which *lingzhi* and pine trees grow, a four-character inscription on one of the rock faces reading: "The ancient immortal is deeply [cultivated] in the Way and its virtues."

Attributed to Suzhou

1780-1850
Height: 5.6 cm

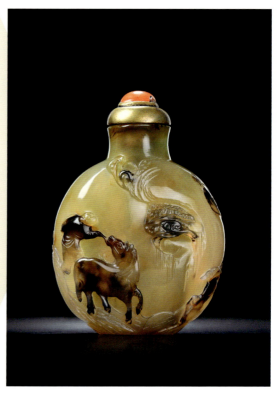

附：清　瑪瑙巧雕蘇作靈猴攀桃牌

蘇瑪瑙牌呈長方板片狀，兩面雕工，屬蘇作工。一面利用天然俏色高浮雕靈猴攀桃，靈猴與斜出的桃枝以深褐色質地突出表現，對比背景的清透感，尤顯主題鮮明。另一面則以浮雕技法，刻畫重巒巨崖，右側留白處署「山果屬猴公」五字。

1780-1850年
高：5.7 厘米

An agate pendant, of flattened rectangular shape with rounded corners; of pale gray, honey-brown and dark brown tones; carved on one main side in relief using the darker colors as a cameo with a monkey seated in a rocky landscape, his arm reaching out to clutch a branch of ripe peaches, a bat in flight above the monkey; the reverse with an inscription reading: "Mountain fruits belong to the Monkey King."

Attributed to Suzhou

1780-1850
Height: 5.7 cm

一面雕：
「山果屬猴公」

87

清　瑪瑙巧雕人物故事蘇作鼻煙壺

鼻煙壺整料天然瑪瑙雕成，呈扁瓶形。直口，溜肩，弧腹，腹下漸收，橢圓形圈足。屬蘇作工。通體淺褐色，一面利用深褐色塊斑，巧雕一人物在童僕的協助下，作翻牆狀，左側門楣上有「花園」二字。其圖像內涵正是描寫《西廂記》中張生翻牆企圖與崔鶯鶯幽會的情節。另一面同樣以局部巧雕技法，摹刻張良幫黃石公撿拾鞋子的場景，左方留白處並署「綺（杞）橋三進履」五字。

1800-1880年
高：5.7 厘米

An agate bottle, very well hollowed; of flattened, rounded form with a cylindrical neck and a neatly carved oval footrim; of honey-brown and dark brown tones; carved on one main side in relief using the darker colors as a cameo within a circular panel with two figures on a bridge beside massive rockwork, looking down at the water, a two-character seal to one side reading: 'Yiyuan' ("Art Garden"); the reverse with a figure holding a box seated on the bridge with his attendant to one side, a five-character inscription above them reading: "[Zhang Liang] picking up the shoe three times at the Yi Bridge, Yiyuan."

Attributed to Suzhou

1800-1880
Height: 5.7 cm

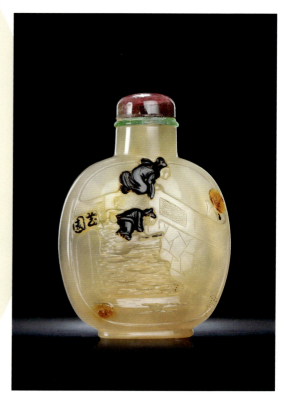

附：清　瑪瑙巧雕蘇作牧馬嘶風牌

瑪瑙牌呈長方板片狀，兩面雕工，屬蘇作工。通體在淡黃色質地上利用深褐色塊斑巧雕裝飾紋樣，一面雕一黑馬抬足前行，牧童立於黑馬前作引導貌。另一面著重刻劃重巒巨岩，巨岩上並題有「牧馬嘶風」四字。

1780-1850年
高：4.5 厘米

An agate pendant, of flattened rectangular shape with rounded corners; of pale gray, honey-brown and dark brown tones; carved on one main side in relief using the darker colors as a cameo with a figure walking through rocky terrain beside a pine tree, followed by his horse; the reverse with a raised inscription reading: "The horse neighs into the wind", beside a craggy rock, all surrounded by serrated rockwork.

Attributed to Suzhou

1780-1850
Height: 4.5 cm

88

清　瑪瑙巧雕「蘇武牧羊」蘇作鼻煙壺

鼻煙壺天然瑪瑙雕成，呈扁瓶形。直口，溜肩，弧腹，腹下漸收，底部微凹。屬蘇作工。通體淺黃色，兩面利用局部褐色塊斑，巧雕「蘇武牧羊」圖，圖作通景式，一面飾群羊安詳於荒野食草，蘇武持杖坐於石上，左側署「蘇武牧羊」四字。另一面局部雕飾巨岩危崖，表現北方蕭瑟無人的地理環境，留白處刻有：「朔雪滿天，飛鴻入漢關，麒麟閣在幸生還。」十六字詩句。

1800-1880年
高：6.2 厘米

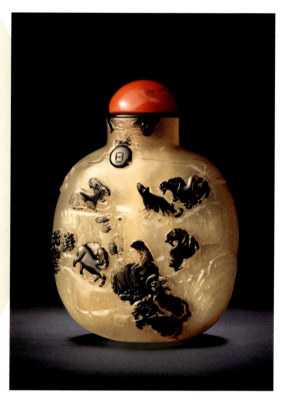

An agate bottle, very well hollowed, of rounded bulbous form with a cylindrical neck, and a flat oval foot; of honey-brown and dark brown tones; carved on one main side in relief using the darker colors as a cameo with a scene of a herd of goats grazing on rocky outcrops beneath the sun high in the sky, a four-character inscription to one side reading: "Su Wu tending the sheep"; the reverse with serrated rockwork with dendritic inclusions resembling a line of trees, an inscription to one side reading:

"Heavy snow from the North fills up the entrance,
where the flying goose enters Han,
enshrined in the Tower of Qilin,
it was fortunate Su Wu returned alive."
the shoulders with a mantle of scrolling clouds.

Attributed to Suzhou

1800-1880
Height: 6.2 cm

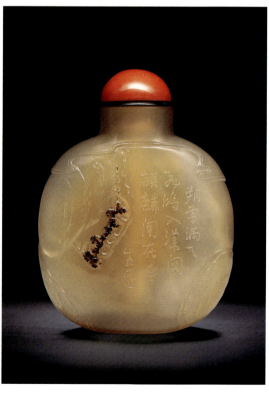

一面左側署：
「蘇武牧羊」

另一面雕刻：
「朔雪滿天，
飛鴻入漢關。
麒麟閣在幸生還。」

附：清　瑪瑙巧雕蘇作西廂記牌

蘇作黃瑪瑙牌呈橢圓形板片狀，通體黃色，兩面雕工。皆以剔地技法浮雕蕉葉亭園人物，圖作通景式，一面像是以遠景鏡頭，雕飾庭園人物；一面則是如鏡頭特寫，可見庭園內洞石蕉葉。唯一不變的是圖中人物的比例大小，鮮明強調《西廂記》中的情愛橋段。

1780-1850年
高：5.7 厘米

A carnelian pendant, of flattened, oval shape, of vivid orange tones; carved in relief on one main side, with women in a walled garden surrounded by trees, and serrated rockwork; the reverse with two figures in conversation, one seated, beside rockwork, the other standing in the shade of a banana tree.

Attributed to Suzhou

1780-1850
Height: 5.7 cm

89

清　瑪瑙巧雕「漁翁得利」蘇作鼻煙壺

鼻煙壺天然瑪瑙雕成，略呈圓罐形。直口，溜肩，深腹，腹下近底部漸收，平底。屬蘇作工。通體紅褐色，利用深褐色塊斑巧雕漁樵樂事。圖作通景式，一漁翁立於江舟上，手中的釣竿正釣起一尾肥美的江魚，歡樂的瞬間似乎也引起樹上禽鳥的覷覦，而岸上的松蔭間，雉雞咕咕逡巡，營造出與世無爭的漁家樂事。

1800-1880年
高：6 厘米

An agate bottle, well hollowed; of bulbous ovoid form with a cylindrical neck, and a flat oval foot, of gray, honey-brown and dark brown tones; continuously carved in relief using the darker colors as a cameo with a scene of a fisherman in a sampan on the river under a pine tree, casting his rod into the water, a peacock perched behind him; the reverse with craggy rocks and pine trees.

Attributed to Suzhou

1800-1880
Height: 6 cm

附：清　瑪瑙巧雕蘇作蓬萊仙境牌

瑪瑙牌呈長方板片狀，通體淡灰褐色，兩面雕工，屬蘇作工。一面利用深褐色塊斑浮雕李白飲酒賦詩圖，李白坐於松巖下，前有橫軸開展，旁有美酒一罈，右上方留白處署「飲酒賦詩」四字。另一面則利用淺褐色局部皮紋，巧雕劉海戲蟾，劉海立於滔浪岸邊，下垂一貫金錢與金蟾，具仙風道骨之姿。左側留白處，署「蓬萊仙境」四字。

1780-1850年
高：6 厘米

An agate pendant, of flattened rectangular shape with rounded corners; of pale gray, honey-brown and dark brown tones; carved on one main side in relief using the darker colors as a cameo with a rocky landscape with two figures seated on a rock under a pine tree, beside a towering rock with a four-character inscription incised on one face reading: "Drink wine and compose poems", a *lingzhi* growing from a craggy rock; the reverse with a third figure in flowing robes seated before a massive rock with an inscription on one face reading: "In the heavenly realm of Penglai"; a border of scrolling clouds at the top.

Attributed to Suzhou

1780-1850
Height: 6 cm

玉雕山水鼻煙壺

在中國瓷器中，「玉雕山水」(Master of the rocks) 一詞並不為亞洲藏家熟知，這詞彙由西方學者提出，專指一組特殊的瓷器。我們一般把「玉雕山水」流派的瓷器定為過渡期晚期至康熙早期，創作於1644-1690年間的作品。這風格見於青花器物，當時工匠受到同期畫家，如董其昌（1555-1636年）等影響，用繪畫的技藝描繪瓷器上的山水畫片。曾經，這被誤認為是某一作坊的特殊風格，但根據大量實物，我們發現這些設計與繪製出自多人之手。

說到鼻煙壺，「玉雕山水」流派一般用於形容青白玉帶皮鼻煙壺，皮色多為紅棕色，深淺不一。這類鼻煙壺曾被稱為漢派。這個流派主要雕山水紋樣，層巒疊翠、流水潺潺、亭台樓閣，工匠利用玉皮增強對比效果。同時，也有其他題材，如雙龍捧壽、傲雪寒梅等。這個流派的精品，可與名聲更響的蘇作在工藝、美學、石材運用上相媲美。

MASTER OF THE ROCKS SCHOOL

In Chinese porcelain, the phrase 'Master of the Rocks' style is not familiar to Asian collectors as it is an invented category used in the west to label a group of porcelain wares. Master of the Rocks style porcelain pieces are usually dated to the late Transitional or early Kangxi period, around 1644 to 1690. This style is characterized on underglaze blue and white porcelain by the depiction of mountainous landscapes in a painterly style and was inspired by late Ming painters such as Dong Qichang (1555-1636). It has been suggested that the style was the work of one ceramic workshop, but examination of these porcelain wares indicates that more than one hand was involved in the design and execution of these pieces.

In the snuff bottle world, the Master of the Rocks School is a term used to describe jade snuff bottles generally of a celadon-green tone which are partially covered with a russet-brown skin of varying thicknesses. It was once known as the 'Han School.' The school's main output was landscape designs where the carver used the dark brown skin of the jade to great effect in the distinctive carving of pavilions nestled in pine trees by a river, set in a mountainous landscape with jagged peaks and waterfalls. However, other subjects are recorded such as confronted dragons surrounding a *shou* medallion and blossoming prunus branches growing from a jagged rockface. At its best, the Master of the Rocks School is every bit the equal of the better known Suzhou School in terms of technical quality, artistry, and in the impressive use of the natural elements of the stone.

90

清　黃玉帶皮巧雕「羲之愛鵝」鼻煙壺

鼻煙壺整料和闐黃玉雕成，局部有褐色斑。通體作扁瓶形，直口，溜肩，弧腹，腹下漸收，橢圓形圈足。全器滿工，腹壁一面利用皮色巧雕羲之愛鵝，羲之立於松樹蕉葉下的水塘邊，正與童僕和行鵝嬉戲，畫面溫煦祥和。另一面以陰刻技法雕祥雲行龍，行龍藏身如意雲紋間，形象威猛，具皇家氣勢。又兩側面亦充分利用皮色，巧雕屈身夔龍。

是件鼻煙壺，玉色甜美，造型飽滿，雕工精細，是一件不可多得的掌中佳器。

1780-1850年
高：6.5 厘米

A nephrite bottle, very well hollowed; of celadon green tone with a russet and dark brown skin; of flattened ovoid form, with shoulders sloping to a cylindrical neck, and with a neatly carved oval footrim, carved on one main side using the skin as a cameo with an attendant bringing a goose to his master who is seated on a rock in a mountainous landscape, a pot in front of him, with pine trees, banana trees, and *lingzhi* growing amongst the massive rockwork, with scrolling clouds which continue onto the reverse of the bottle, partially hiding a coiling scaly dragon flying through the clouds; the two narrow sides with formalized archaistic dragons.

Master of the Rocks School

1780-1850
Height: 6.5 cm

91

清　黃玉帶皮巧雕「和合二仙」鼻煙壺

鼻煙壺整料和闐黃玉雕成，呈扁瓶形，局部有褐色斑。直口，
溜肩，扁腹，腹下近底部漸收，橢圓形圈足。一面利用褐色皮
巧雕和合二仙，二仙作童子捧盒貌，泛舟江海，其中一人的手
中捧盒竄出祥雲且直上雲霄，鮮明刻劃「和合二仙」的藝術形
象。另一面則光素無紋，一任展現黃玉質地的溫潤之美。

1780-1850年
高：6.3 厘米

A nephrite bottle, very well hollowed; of yellowish-green
tone with a russet and dark brown skin; of flattened
ovoid form, with shoulders sloping to a cylindrical neck,
and with a neatly carved oval footrim; carved on one
main side using the skin as a cameo with two figures in
a log-boat on waves, one seated and holding an incense
burner from which vapor rises into the scrolling clouds
above them; the reverse left uncarved to highlight the
patch of russet skin towards the base resembling a
flowering shrub.

Master of the Rocks School

1780-1850
Height: 6.3 cm

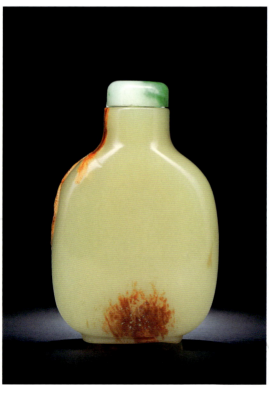

清　黃玉帶皮巧雕「明月松間照」鼻煙壺

鼻煙壺整料和闐黃玉雕成，呈扁瓶形，局部有褐色斑。直口，溜肩，深腹，腹下近底部漸收，橢圓形圈足。一面利用褐色玉皮，浮雕參天老松，老松屈曲遒勁，恣意顯露春天般的無窮生機。又老松頂端因飾有雲掩明月如詩境「明月松間照」。另一面打磨光亮，一任光素，刻意表現如嬰兒般的細膩玉質。

1780-1850年
高：5.9 厘米

A nephrite bottle, very well hollowed; of yellowish-green tone with a russet-brown skin; of rectangular form, with rounded shoulders sloping to a cylindrical neck, and with a neatly carved oval footrim, carved on one main side using the skin as a cameo with a gnarly pine tree beside towering rockwork and under scrolling clouds; the reverse left uncarved.

Master of the Rocks School

1780-1850
Height: 5.9 cm

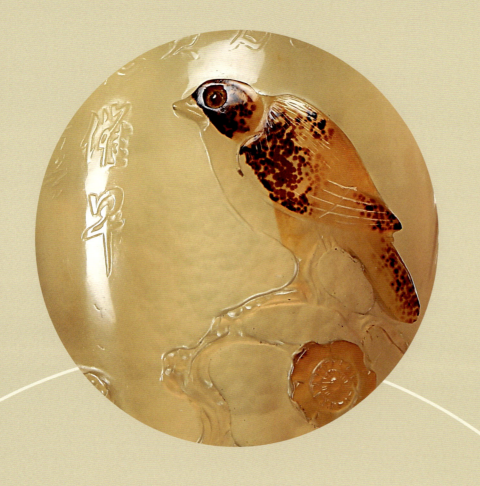

官樣

瑪瑙

非宮廷的瑪瑙鼻煙壺大多創作於1750-1860年間。十八世紀五十年代，鼻煙壺在宮外受到文人與富裕的藏家所追捧。1860年為咸豐皇帝晚期，當時中國深陷太平天國運動，清朝國庫虧空，這導致藝術與手工業在景德鎮等地區逐漸瓦解，當地眾多生產瓷器的窯口毀於一旦。

瑪瑙是石英的一種，質地細緻，其化學成分為二氧化矽，硬度為7，比重為2.6-2.7。因此它比玉硬，但比海藍寶、綠柱石、碧璽、紅寶石和藍寶石等軟。雖然紅寶石和藍寶石鼻煙壺罕見，但它們屬於剛玉，硬度較高，又稱「解玉砂」，在製作玉鼻煙壺和瑪瑙鼻煙壺時，用於進行碾磨和拋光。

瑪瑙是一種呈帶狀的顏色豐富的玉髓。其顏色和紋理多種多樣，因此無法找到兩件一模一樣的瑪瑙鼻煙壺。作為石材，瑪瑙的獨特性與唯一性深深的吸引了十八世紀的收藏家。在成岩過程中，它由眾多圓形結節組成，橫向切開後可窺見其隱藏的內部紋理。

優秀的工匠會根據石材來設計作品，有的不會添加多餘的裝飾，讓觀者得以欣賞石材本身；有的會根據石頭的內含物來設計紋飾，以展示其精湛的雕刻技藝。現存的瑪瑙鼻煙壺大多品質一流，特別是皮影瑪瑙，最是引人入勝。製作皮影瑪瑙一般需要進行打磨去掉部分皮殼來凸顯畫片，但最好的精品只需稍做打磨，其畫片便呈現出來，栩栩如生。

皮影瑪瑙與雕刻瑪瑙鼻煙壺涵蓋了中國文化幾乎所有的紋樣主題，如瑞獸、龍紋、人物、風景。傳統上，這些鼻煙壺被分為兩類。但這種分類讓我們無法欣賞到這些精品的藝術精髓。瑪瑙雕刻大師們最厲害之處是如何一眼相中一塊石材的特點，並據此進行雕刻與打磨。最好的方法不是故意雕刻一個具體的畫片，而是引導觀者去體會其中的奧秘。

「眼球瑪瑙」(eyeball agate) 一詞是莫仕為 (Hugh Moss) 於二十世紀七十年代所創造出來的鼻煙壺詞彙。專指利用瑪瑙本身帶狀同心環來表現主體的眼睛，常見的有鳥、魚，少見的有馬、人物等。這組作品，只通過最少的打磨來塑造皮影效果，但其畫片又十分清晰。

莫仕為在二十世紀九十年代創造了「官樣」(Official School) 一詞，後被廣泛使用。在某些情況下，通過紋飾的主題來劃分鼻煙壺是很有用的，但不意味著劃分出來的鼻煙壺屬同一時期於同一作坊生產。此外，類別有時會有重疊，例如我們可以同時把某一鼻煙壺歸為官樣與蘇州流派。

在中國宮廷的官僚體系裏，鼻煙壺是一個完美的社交與政治媒介，用於討好並獲取權貴青睞，或用於對所受恩惠表達感謝。那些身居高位、名聲顯赫的貴人通過把鼻煙壺當作禮物贈送給下屬來彰顯其身份。中國藝術品可在多層維度上與藏家對話。其中比較簡單是紋飾的寓意，舉一個例子，畫片中繪有一隻猴子騎在馬背上，旁設一隻蜜蜂，有時可能沒有蜜蜂，均有「馬上封侯」一祝願對方立即升官之意。大多情況下，蜜蜂被繪於馬的右側。這類鼻煙壺便是給有志之士的最佳禮物，現今我們常把它們歸為「官樣」。

OFFICIAL SCHOOL

Agate

Most agate bottles without an imperial designation are dated within the range of 1750-1860. The beginning date is given as a time when the popularity of snuff bottles began to climb and spread outside the Court to both scholars and wealthy connoisseurs. The cut-off date is almost at the end of the Xianfeng period when the country was in turmoil with the Taiping Rebellion, the near bankruptcy of the Imperial Court, and the resulting disintegration of art and craft in areas such as Jingdezhen, where the kilns for ceramic production had been destroyed.

Agate comes under the grouping of quartz and is specifically microcrystalline quartz whose composition is silicon dioxide. It has a hardness of 7 and a specific gravity of 2.6 - 2.7. This makes it slightly harder than jade, and softer than gemstones such as aquamarine, beryl, tourmaline, ruby, and sapphire. The last two are relevant because although there are not many snuff bottles in these materials, their composition is conundrum, which is used as part of the grinding compound of the lapidary in the carving and polishing of both jades and agates.

Agate is a banded, multi-colored variety of chalcedony. It occurs in a boundless amount of colors and patterns and, as such, no two agate bottles will ever be identical. As a stone, the extraordinary beauty and uniqueness of agate were responsible for its great popularity with collectors from the eighteenth century onwards. In the rock, it forms in rounded nodules, which must be sliced open to reveal the hidden internal patterns.

The great carver can allow this to be enjoyed by those who can simply appreciate the stone itself without any further adornment or it can be carved to great effect with subjects that are suggested by the inclusions in the stone itself. There is a wide range of agate bottles but those that reach a stellar quality, especially in the case of silhouette agate bottles are the most exciting of snuff bottles. It is often necessary to polish into the surface to enhance the scene, but with the best of these examples only slight polishing is necessary to give a clear definition to the whole identifiable picture.

Both silhouette and carved agate bottles cover the whole sphere of Chinese culture through their subject matter such as mythical beasts, the ever-present dragon, figures, and scenes of contemplation. Traditionally these types of bottles have been separated into two groups. However, these divisions detract from the sheer artistry of the best of these bottles. One of the great abilities that the master carvers of the genre had, was the expertise to pick a moment in the stone and cut and polish it. This is best done in such a way that it does not force a scene but simply encourages the eye to see what the mind wants to suggest.

The term "eyeball agate" was a phrase coined in the 1970s by Hugh Moss and is specific to snuff bottles. It refers to agate bottles with smaller concentric rings depicting the eye of the subject matter, usually birds or fish, and on occasion horses or human figures. With this group, the design is very clear although the silhouette has usually been achieved by a minimal amount of polishing.

The Official School is an accepted term for a group of quartz bottles since its invention in the 1990s by Hugh Moss. In some cases, it is useful to be able to label bottles according to their subject matter. However, this does not necessarily infer that all of these bottles were made at the same time in the same workshop. Additionally, some groups overlap and it is possible, for example, to attribute a bottle to both the Official School and the Suzhou School.

Within the Chinese bureaucratic system of the court, the snuff bottle was the perfect vehicle to be used socially and politically to curry favor, to gain an audience to those in power, and to show appreciation for favors received. Those who had gained rank and prestige were able to show their superiority by dispensing snuff bottles as gifts to those beneath them. Chinese art spoke to connoisseurs on many different levels of communication. At a fairly simple level was the idea of a rebus, which works as follows: the depiction of a monkey on the back of a horse with or without a wasp infers "may you be immediately appointed to a high ranking position" through the phrase *Mashang fenghou*. In most cases where there is a wasp depicted, it is shown on the right-hand side of the horse. A bottle such as this would have been perceived as the ideal gift for an aspiring official, and would today be categorized as being part of the Official School.

93

清　羊肝瑪瑙巧雕「一定封侯」鼻煙壺

鼻煙壺整料天然瑪瑙雕成，通體羊肝色質地，局部有黃、褐色皮。直口，豐肩，弧腹，腹下近底部漸收，橢圓形圈足。一面利用俏色雕一坐於蕉蔭湖石上的靈猴，靈猴手中持一棍棒，向一旁的蜜蜂飛舞，代表「一定封侯」的吉祥寓意。另一面打磨光素，惟瑪瑙的天然紋樣，似乎隱隱有月下湖色的迷濛景象，令人激賞。

1780-1850年
高：6.8 厘米

A jasper bottle, well hollowed; of ochre, olive-green and russet tones; of bulbous, rounded form, with rounded shoulders sloping to a cylindrical neck, and with a neatly carved oval footrim, carved on one main side with a monkey seated on a rock beside a banana tree brandishing a stick at a wasp flying above it; the reverse left uncarved, allowing the beige inclusion to resemble the sun high in the sky.

Official School

1780-1850
Height: 6.8 cm

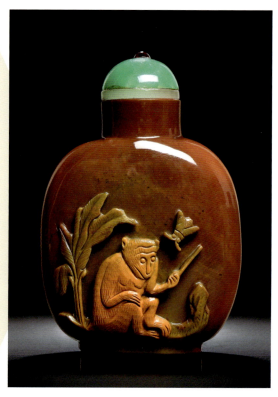

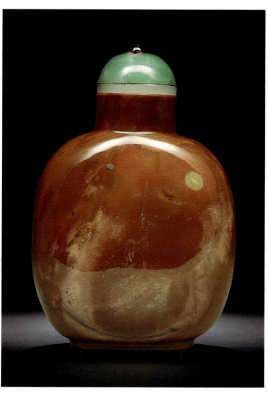

94

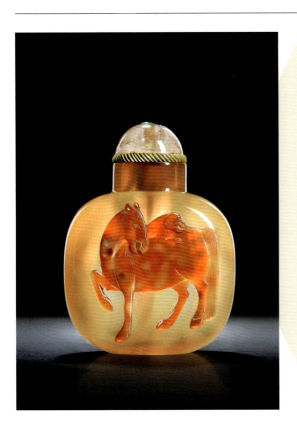

清　瑪瑙巧雕「馬上封侯」鼻煙壺

鼻煙壺整料天然瑪瑙雕成，淺褐色質地，局部有深褐色斑。通體作扁瓶形。直口，豐肩，弧腹，腹下近底部漸收，橢圓形淺圈足。一面利用俏色巧雕一翹足而行的立馬，馬背上攀附一靈猴，靈猴面容討喜可愛，增添「馬上封侯」的吉祥寓意。背面打磨光素，不施任何裝飾紋樣，讓瑪瑙的天然美肌一覽無遺。

1780-1850年
高：5.2 厘米

An agate bottle, superbly hollowed; of honey-brown tone with a dappled brown inclusion; of bulbous, rounded form, with rounded shoulders sloping to a cylindrical neck, and with a flat oval foot, carved on one main side with a horse with one leg raised, turning its head to observe the monkey on its back; the reverse left uncarved.

Official School

1780-1850
Height: 5.2 cm

95

清　瑪瑙巧雕「旗開得勝」鼻煙壺

鼻煙壺天然瑪瑙雕成，通體淡灰褐色質地，局部有紅褐色斑。
呈扁瓶形。直口，溜肩，弧腹，腹下近底部漸收，橢圓形圈
足。正面利用紅色皮，巧雕「旗開得勝」圖，圖中一馬作奔馳
貌，坐於馬背上的傳令手持一隨風飄揚的令旗，故稱「旗開得
勝」。本件鼻煙壺的背面亦作光素，惟前述傳令帽上的翎羽作
水平飄浮，恰是表現快馬速度感的畫龍點睛之筆。

1780-1850年
高：5.9 厘米

An agate bottle, superbly hollowed; of pale brown tone
with a dappled honey-brown inclusion; of bulbous,
rounded form, with rounded shoulders sloping to a
cylindrical neck, and with a neatly carved oval footrim;
carved on one main side with a Manchu bannerman
astride a galloping horse, his banner flying over one
shoulder; the reverse left uncarved.

Official School

1780-1850
Height: 5.9 cm

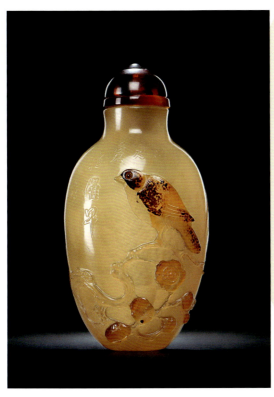

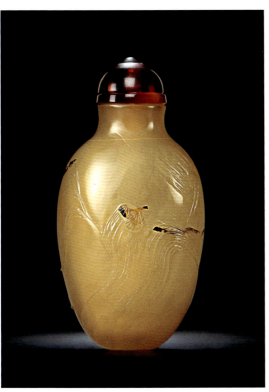

96

清　瑪瑙巧雕「喜上眉梢」鼻煙壺

鼻煙壺天然瑪瑙雕成，略作圓罐形。直口，溜肩，深腹，腹下漸收，橢圓形平底。通體於淺褐色地淺雕自山岩間斜出屈曲的梅枝，梅枝上綻放朵花與待放含苞相互爭豔，枝頭上並停佇一隻喜鵲，喜鵲、朵花以深褐色塊斑凸顯，越發強化「喜上眉梢」的吉祥寓意。腹壁留白處，並署有「又見黃梅催早春」詩句。

1780-1850年
高：6.5 厘米

An agate bottle, very well hollowed; of honey-brown tone with dappled brown inclusions; of bulbous, ovoid form, with rounded shoulders sloping to a cylindrical neck with a slightly everted mouth, and with a flat oval foot, carved on one main side with a bird of prey perched on the twisted branch of a blossoming *Huang Mei* tree, an inscription to one side reading: "Yellow prunus is seen, heralding another early spring", the reverse left uncarved.

Official School

1780-1850
Height: 6.5 cm

其他 MISCELLANEOUS

- 玉 Jade
- 瑪瑙 Agate
- 其他物料 Various Materials

97

清　黃玉巧雕「子孫萬代」鼻煙壺

鼻煙壺和闐黃玉雕成，局部有褐色斑，作葫蘆形。直口，束腰，上垂腹，下鼓腹，平底。葫蘆外浮雕藤蔓纏繞，藤蔓上的葉子以俏色表現，增添色彩變化。又蔓葉上並有小葫蘆垂掛。由於葫蘆多籽，而蔓帶可諧音萬代，因此本件鼻煙壺遂有「子孫萬代」的美好寓意。

1750-1820年
高：5.9 厘米

A nephrite bottle, very well hollowed; of yellow tone with a brown inclusion; of double gourd form sloping to a cylindrical neck; with double gourds and leafy scrolling vines continuously carved in relief around the bottle.

1750-1820
Height: 5.9 cm

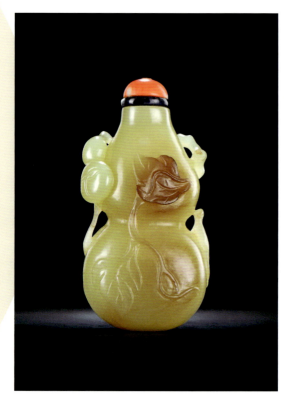

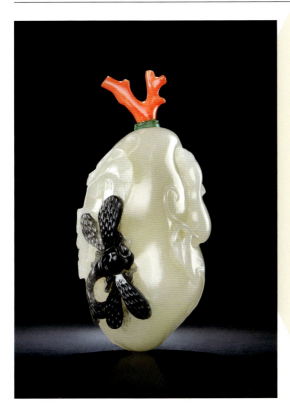

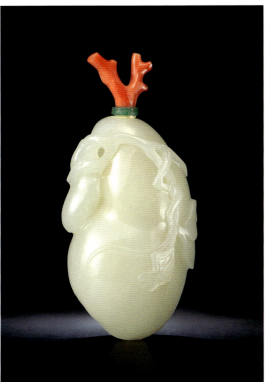

清　黑白玉巧雕「萬代清福」鼻煙壺

鼻煙壺整料和闐玉雕成，玉色白中帶黑，通體作象生葫蘆。亮點之處是利用黑色質地，浮雕蜻蜓停佇葫蘆上，葫蘆外壁亦浮雕有蔓葉和小葫蘆，此間葫蘆代表萬代，而蜻蜓在圖像意象中，亦常與「清福」連結，因此本件鼻煙壺被賦予「萬代清福」的表徵，也就不在話下。

1750-1820年
高：6 厘米

A nephrite bottle, very well hollowed; of white tone with a dark-gray inclusion; of double gourd form; with a dragonfly flying among double gourds and leafy scrolling vines continuously carved in relief around the bottle.

1750-1820
Height: 6 cm

99

清　白玉帶皮光素鼻煙壺

鼻煙壺整料和闐白玉雕成，玉色潔白，凝密溫潤。通體扁瓶
形。直口，豐肩，弧腹，腹下近底部漸收，橢圓形圈足。全器
不施任何裝飾紋樣，且刻意保留了幾佔腹壁一半的紅褐色皮，
由於皮色鮮豔可人，縱使沒有紋樣的形象連結，是件鼻煙壺猶
有「紅透半邊天」的摩登意趣。

1750-1800年
高：6.2 厘米

A nephrite bottle, very well hollowed; of even white tone
with a russet-brown skin on one side; of ovoid form with
rounded shoulders and a cylindrical neck, and with a
neatly carved oval footrim; one main side with the skin
polished to form an irregular natural design on half of
the surface.

1750-1800
Height: 6.2 cm

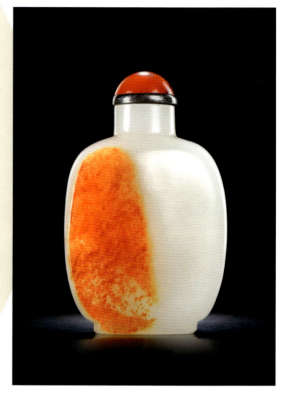

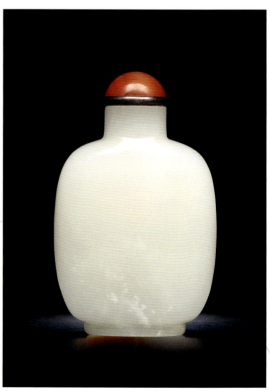

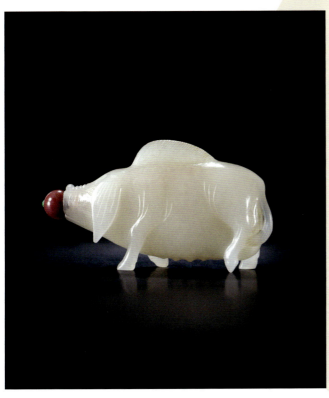

清　白玉山豬形鼻煙壺

鼻煙壺整料白玉雕成，玉質水漾，白皙透裡。通體作肖生山豬形，是豬體態肥壯，背脊起一排豎鬃毛，腹下出兩排乳頭，四肢作行走貌，兩尖耳垂覆於頸肩兩側，吻部微噘。全器造型刻劃逼真，比例線條優美，除予人形象藝術的饗宴外，又因豬蹄的蹄與題同音，故也有「雁塔題名」的吉祥寓意。

1750-1800年
長：5.7 厘米

A nephrite bottle, very well hollowed; of even white tone; carved with finely incised details in the form of a plump trotting sow, one hoof raised, her tail curled around her hindquarters, the belly with small udders.

1750-1800
Length: 5.7 cm

101

清　白玉鹿形鼻煙壺

鼻煙壺整料白玉雕成，玉質溫潤潔白，作肖生鹿形。是鹿呈跪臥狀，頭微昂，橄欖形小眼，鼻出小孔，口微啟，雙耳後翹，長角貼背，腹部滿佈米字紋，小尾垂臀，四肢收於腹下。是件鼻煙壺造型寫實，形象鮮活，置臥鹿於掌上，似乎也有掌握官祿，封官進爵之意。

1750-1800年
長：5.6 厘米

A nephrite bottle, very well hollowed; of even white tone; carved with finely incised details in the form of a reclining deer, with its legs tucked underneath its body and its antlers laid back against its shoulders.

1750-1800
Length: 5.6 cm

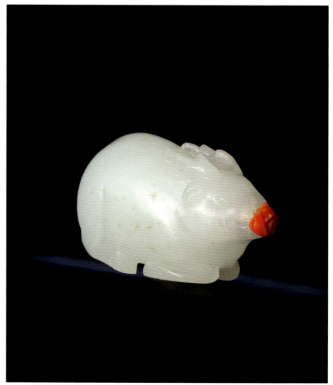

102

清　白玉雕花卉紋鼻煙壺

鼻煙壺整料白玉雕成，局部有褐色斑，作扁瓶形。直口，溜肩，弧腹，腹下漸收，平底。腹壁兩面開光，開光內磨砂地，砂地上分別飾壓地隱起折枝牡丹與折枝菊花。兩肩側面亦起立式橢圓形開光，開光內分別飾以蘭花與修竹。全器雕工精緻，紋樣清雅，具文人書卷氣息。

1750-1800年
高：5.6 厘米

A nephrite bottle, very well hollowed; of even white tone with a small patch of russet-brown skin; of flattened, rounded form with a cylindrical neck and a neatly carved oval footrim; carved on one main side within a circular panel with a leafy, flowering chrysanthemum; the reverse carved with a peony; the two narrow sides carved with raised oval panels, one carved with a lily, the other with an orchid.

1750-1800
Height: 5.6 cm

103

清　白玉雕石榴紋鼻煙壺

鼻煙壺整料和闐白玉雕成，玉質細密凝膩，作扁瓶形。直口，溜肩，弧腹，腹下漸收，平底。通體作瓜棱腹，枝葉斜出，腹壁一端露出球形果實，故知為石榴。石榴多子，以石榴入形，自有「多子多孫」的吉祥寓意。

1750-1800年
高：5.2 厘米

A nephrite bottle, very well hollowed; of even white tone; of bulbous, rounded form with shoulders sloping to a cylindrical neck, and with a flat oval foot, carved in the form of a ripe pomegranate bursting with seeds, and with leafy tendrils continuously carved in relief around the fruit.

1750-1800
Height: 5.2 cm

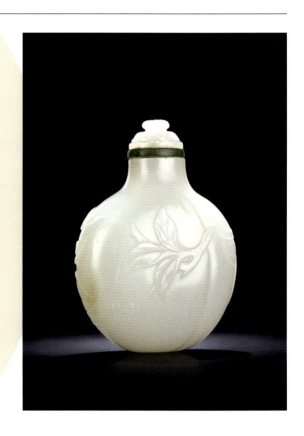

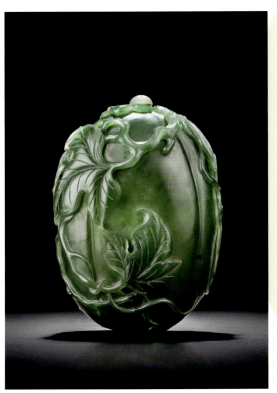

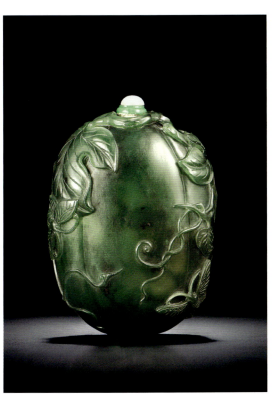

104

清　碧玉雕「瓜瓞綿綿」鼻煙壺

鼻煙壺整料瑪納斯碧玉雕成，玉色碧綠，色調均勻，肌理略有黑斑。通體作瓜果形，造型飽滿，蔓葉纏繞於腹壁，線條流轉，舒展有度。腹壁一端亦飾有蝴蝶翩翩飛舞，而蝶與瓞（小瓜之意）諧音，以致是件鼻煙壺的「瓜瓞綿綿」造型，自有表徵「子孫綿延」的吉祥寓意。

1759-1800年
高：6.2 厘米

A nephrite bottle, very well hollowed; of spinach-green tones; carved in the form of a plump melon with a butterfly among leafy vines and tendrils continuously carved in relief around the fruit.

1759-1800
Height: 6.2 cm

清　白玉雕「瓜瓞綿綿」鼻煙壺

鼻煙壺整料和闐白玉雕成，玉質潔白姣好，作瓜形。全器
裝飾紋樣與前述碧玉鼻煙壺大抵雷同，俱是以「瓜」與
「蝶」的意象，表徵「瓜瓞綿綿」之意。不過相同之中亦
有小異，仔細分辨，本件鼻煙壺的瓜形似為茄瓜類，通體
較為修長，尾端收尖錐，呈現類似題材中，多樣化的賞玩
趣味。

1750-1800年
高：6.3 厘米

A nephrite bottle, very well hollowed; of even white tone; carved in the form of a plump melon with leafy vines and tendrils continuously carved in relief around the fruit.

1750-1800
Height: 6.3 cm

106

清　白玉雕「子孫萬代」鼻煙壺

鼻煙壺整料和闐白玉雕成，玉質凝潤，作象生瓠瓜。瓠瓜微束腰，外壁以高浮雕技法剔飾蔓葉纏繞，其間梗葉扶疏，並有數棵小葫蘆纍纍垂掛。通體雕工精細，線條流暢，以藝術寫形，同時也完美傳達了「子孫萬代」的吉祥寓意。

1750-1820年
高：5.8 厘米

A nephrite bottle, very well hollowed; of even white tone; carved in the form of a ripened, plump double gourd with double gourds and leafy scrolling vines continuously carved in relief around the bottle, the bottle standing on feet fashioned as double gourds.

1750-1820
Height: 5.8 cm

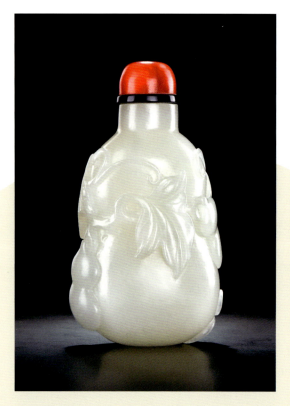

107

清　白玉雕「福祿萬代」鼻煙壺

鼻煙壺和闐白玉雕成，玉色白皙，溫潤凝滑。通體作瓠瓜形。
直口，中腰微束，外壁以浮雕技法飾藤蔓纏繞，蔓葉翻捲開
闔，與大小葫蘆勾藤垂掛相映成趣。全器造型飽滿，惟瓠瓜一
側因飾有一蝙蝠意象，故鼻煙壺也被賦予「福祿萬代」的美好
想望。

1750-1820年
高：6.5厘米

A nephrite bottle, very well hollowed; of even white tone; carved in the form of a ripened, plump double gourd with a cylindrical neck, with a bat flying among double gourds and leafy scrolling vines continuously carved in relief around the bottle.

1750-1820
Height: 6.5 cm

108

清　白玉帶皮巧雕「多子多孫」鼻煙壺

鼻煙壺和闐白玉雕成，局部有褐色皮斑。通體作扁豆形，外壁
利用皮色巧雕蔓葉纏繞，增添視覺上的色彩變化。枝梗蔓葉上
並有小扁豆垂掛，由於扁豆系多子植物，因此大扁豆、小扁豆
的意象結合，便有「多子多孫」的吉祥表徵。

1750-1820年
高：6.8 厘米

A nephrite bottle, very well hollowed; of even white tone with patches of russet-brown skin; carved in the form of a pea pod swollen with ripe peas, with leafy scrolling vines continuously carved in relief around the bottle, standing on a small circular concave foot.

1750-1820
Height: 6.8 cm

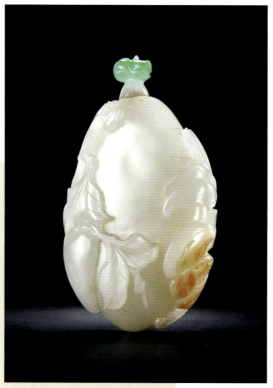

109

清　白玉巧雕「洪福多子」鼻煙壺

鼻煙壺和闐白玉雕成，局部有褐色斑，玉質致密，潔淨白潤。
通體作瓜形，大瓜的外壁復雕飾枝梗斜出，枝梗上並有小瓜纍
纍垂掛。瓜腹一側巧妙以褐色皮俏雕一蝙蝠，紅蝠諧音洪福，
瓜屬多子，故有「洪福多子」的意思。

1750-1820年
高：6.2 厘米

A nephrite bottle, very well hollowed; of even white tone with a patch of russet-brown skin; carved in the form of a ripened, plump gourd with a bat flying among gourds and leafy scrolling vines continuously carved in relief around the bottle.

1750-1820
Height: 6.2 cm

110

清　白玉帶皮巧雕「金玉滿堂」鼻煙壺

鼻煙壺和闐白玉雕成，局部有褐色斑，略呈扁三角形。通體利
用褐色皮於底邊兩側巧雕兩尾金魚，兩金魚之間淺浮雕蓮花一
朵。金魚一左一右、一白一紅，對應鼻煙壺腹壁一抹褐色皮以
及蓮花意象，一幅荷塘春色所演繹的「金玉滿堂、年年有餘」
也就歡樂上場了。

1750-1820年
高：5.7 厘米

A nephrite bottle, very well hollowed; of white tone with
patches of golden-brown skin; of natural pebble form,
continuously carved in relief with a pair of fan-tailed
carp swimming amongst lotus.

1750-1820
Height: 5.7 cm

111

清　白玉巧雕「福壽雙全」鼻煙壺

鼻煙壺和闐白玉雕成，局部有褐色斑，作並蒂雙桃形，器形飽滿。雙桃交接處淺浮雕一蝙蝠，其間枝葉葳蕤，線條流轉，搭配褐色皮斑的巧妙映襯，更添雙桃的靈動氣息。是件鼻煙壺的壺口開於側面，雙桃與蝙蝠的圖像，顯然有「福壽雙全」的吉祥表徵。

1750-1820年
高：6.6 厘米

A nephrite bottle, very well hollowed; of white tone with patches of russet-brown skin; carved in the form of two ripe peaches, with a bat and leafy scrolling vines continuously carved in relief around the bottle.

1750-1820
Height: 6.6 cm

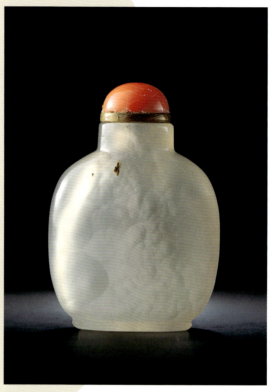

112

清　瑪瑙巧雕「福壽雙全」鼻煙壺

鼻煙壺天然瑪瑙雕成，通體冰糖色，局部有褐色斑。作扁瓶形。直口，溜肩，弧腹，腹下近底部漸收，橢圓形圈足。腹壁一面光素，一面利用深褐色皮斑，淺浮雕一持杖老翁，老翁身著寬袍，長髯，略顯佝僂，可謂將高齡宿耆的形態特徵表露無遺。又老翁背後飾有一蝙蝠，故有「福壽雙全」的美好寓意。

1750-1860年
高：5.5 厘米

An agate bottle, superbly hollowed; of flattened, squared form with rounded shoulders sloping to a cylindrical neck, and with a neatly carved oval footrim; of pale gray tone with honey-brown and dark brown inclusions, lightly carved and polished to depict a bearded figure in flowing robes carrying a long staff, a bat swooping in the air behind him; the reverse left uncarved.

1750-1860
Height: 5.5 cm

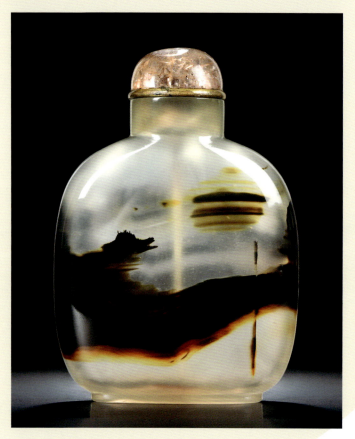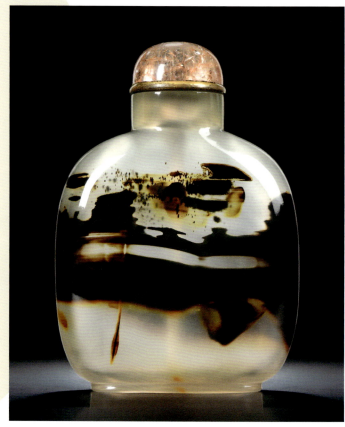

清　影子瑪瑙如潑墨山水「夜泊西湖」「煙雨江南」鼻煙壺

鼻煙壺天然瑪瑙雕成，猶如一幅環繞的潑墨山水畫冰糖瑪瑙地帶褐色斑。
作扁瓶形。直口，溜肩，扁腹，腹下近底部漸收，橢圓形圈足。通體打磨
光素，不施任何紋樣，惟兩面的天然紋理，自有一番風景逸趣。一幅山水景
如「夜泊西湖」，水天一色，孤舟遠影，天水相連，美不勝收。另一面景如
「煙雨江南」，微風吹湖，湖面倒影，煙雨朦朧，淋漓蒼茫，令人神往。兩面
美景不做一刀人為斧鑿，渾然天成，誠讓人拍案叫絕。

1750-1860年
高：8.2 厘米

An agate bottle, superbly hollowed; of flattened, squared form with rounded shoulders sloping to a cylindrical neck, and with a neatly carved oval footrim; of pale gray tone with light brown, honey-brown and dark brown inclusions, resembling an ink-play painting with the silhouette of a continuous mountainous landscape scene of a sampan moored to the banks of a lake with the misty rain falling on the Yangtze River.

1750-1860
Height: 8.2 cm

114

清　影子瑪瑙天然烏鵲紋鼻煙壺

鼻煙壺天然瑪瑙雕成，屬影子瑪瑙，冰糖地帶褐色斑。作扁瓶形。直口，溜肩，扁腹，腹下近底部漸收，橢圓形圈足。通體打磨光素，略做勾勒琢磨，兩面腹壁即因天然的深褐色顯花，而出現烏鵲佇石的有趣畫面。甚至若將一面的褐色圓斑視為水中月影，那麼「月中烏鵲至，花裡鳳凰來」的箇中意境，也就自然浮現眼前了。

1750-1860年
高：5.5 厘米

An agate bottle, superbly hollowed; of flattened, squared form with rounded shoulders sloping to a cylindrical neck, and with a neatly carved oval footrim; of honey-brown tone with dark brown inclusions, lightly carved and polished to depict on one main side the silhouette of a cockerel perched on a rock looking up at the sun in the sky; the reverse with two magpies perched on rocky outcrops looking up into the sky.

1750-1860
Height: 5.5 cm

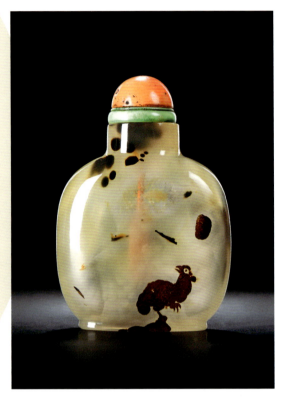

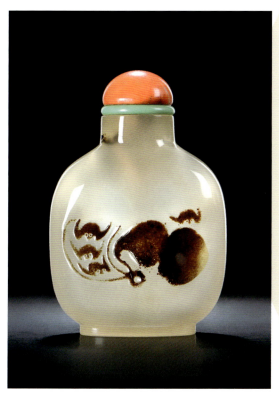

115

清　影子瑪瑙「賜福長壽」鼻煙壺

鼻煙壺天然瑪瑙雕成，屬影子瑪瑙，冰糖地帶褐色斑。作扁瓶形。直口，溜肩，扁腹，腹下近底部漸收，橢圓形圈足。一面打磨光亮，不施任何紋樣；另一面則巧妙利用俏色，巧雕做傾倒狀的葫蘆，葫蘆周圍並附有四隻蝙蝠，而四蝠可諧音賜福，因此也傳達了「賜福長壽」的美好意思。

1750-1860年
高：5.9 厘米

An agate bottle, very well hollowed; of flattened, squared form with rounded shoulders sloping to a cylindrical neck, and with a neatly carved oval footrim; of honey-brown tone with dark brown inclusions, lightly carved and polished to depict on one main side the silhouette of a double gourd issuing bats flying among curling vapors; the reverse plain.

1750-1860
Height: 5.9 cm

116

清　瑪瑙巧雕荷葉金魚鼻煙壺

鼻煙壺天然瑪瑙雕成，通體冰糖色，局部有綠色斑紋。作扁瓶形。直口，溜肩，弧腹，腹下近底部漸收，橢圓形圈足。一面打磨光亮，不施裝飾紋樣；一面利用水草色綠斑紋，巧雕蓮荷金魚，金魚翹尾，做悠游貌，情狀可愛。又蓮荷金魚的綜合意象，不能免俗，也有「年年有餘」的吉祥寓意。

1750-1860年
高：5.5 厘米

An agate bottle, very well hollowed; of flattened, rounded form with shoulders sloping to a cylindrical neck, and with a neatly carved oval footrim; of honey-brown tone with dappled-green inclusions, carved in relief to depict, on one main side, a fan-tailed carp swimming amongst lotus leaves, pods and flowers; the reverse plain.

1750-1860
Height: 5.5 cm

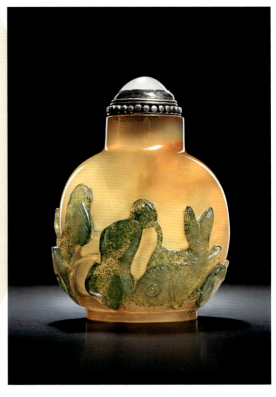

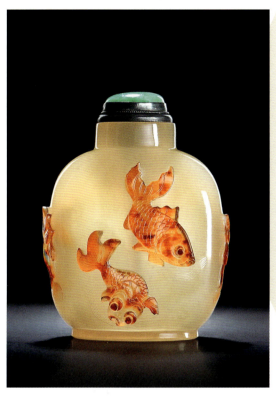

117

清　瑪瑙巧雕「金玉滿堂」鼻煙壺

鼻煙壺天然瑪瑙雕成，通體冰糖色，局部有黃橙斑紋。作扁瓶形。直口，溜肩，弧腹，腹下近底部漸收，橢圓形圈足。一面一任光素，不施任何紋樣；一面則利用褐色皮巧兩尾金魚，腹地局部襯有平行水波紋，兩金魚一呈三葉尾，一做雙葉尾，俱做水中行游貌，予人活靈活現的視覺美感。然兩側肩臂的淺浮雕蓮花紋，亦讓鼻煙壺具有「金玉滿堂、年年有餘」的豐富意象。

1750-1860年
高：5.9 厘米

An agate bottle, very well hollowed; of flattened, rounded form with shoulders sloping to a cylindrical neck, and with a neatly carved oval footrim; of honey-brown tone with vivid dappled-orange inclusions, carved in relief to depict, on one main side, a pair of goldfish, the two narrow sides carved with lotus in low relief; the reverse plain.

1750-1860
Height: 5.9 cm

118

清　紅白瑪瑙巧雕金魚形鼻煙壺

鼻煙壺天然瑪瑙雕成，通體紅白色，作象生魚形。吻部開壺口，水泡眼，嘴銜一束蓮荷，腹部鱗紋刻畫精細，背鰭鮮明，尾部上翹，四周繞以蓮荷。全器顏色鮮麗，造型小巧，刻劃生動，宛如一尾活生生的金魚騰躍於眼前。又金魚與蓮荷的意象，不用多說，自有「年年有餘」的討喜寓意。

1750-1860年
長：5.1 厘米

A carnelian bottle, well hollowed; of vivid orange and white tones; carved in the form of a fish resting on a lotus leaf with lotus blossoms and pods carved in relief, the details finely incised.

1750-1860
Length: 5.1 cm

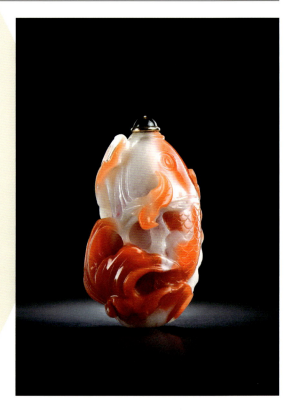

119

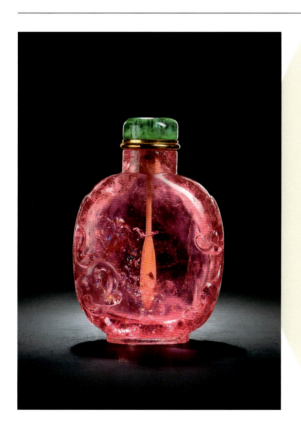

清　碧璽雕雙螭紋鼻煙壺

鼻煙壺天然碧璽雕成，呈半透明桃紅色，肌理可見冰裂紋，具夢幻視覺效果。通體作扁瓶形。直口，溜肩，弧腹，腹下近底部漸收，橢圓形圈足。腹壁兩面光素，兩肩臂淺浮雕二螭龍，螭龍身軀修長，形象鮮活，增添不少全器的靈動氣息。

1800-1900年
高：5.2 厘米

A tourmaline bottle, well hollowed; of vivid bright pink tones; of flattened, ovoid form with rounded shoulders sloping to a cylindrical neck and with a neatly carved oval footrim; carved with two coiling *chilong*.

1800-1900
Height: 5.2 cm

120

清　銀胎開光鏨花鎏金雲龍紋鼻煙壺

鼻煙壺銀質金屬胎，呈扁平形。唇口，短頸，扁圓腹，橢圓形圈足。口緣與肩部各飾一圈連珠紋，腹部兩面以兩圈高低弦紋圍繞成圓形開光，開光內鏨飾鎏金雲龍紋，開光外滿飾鏤空捲草紋。此外，頸部、足壁以及肩臂兩側亦鏨飾淺浮雕捲草紋。全器裝飾華麗，繁縟工整，展現精益求精的皇家氣勢。

1800-1900年
高：6.5 厘米

著錄：耿寶昌主編《中國鼻煙壺珍賞》，（香港）三聯書店，1992年，324頁。

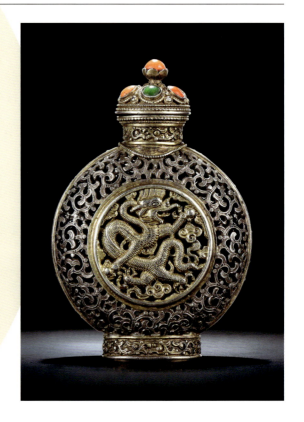

A silver bottle with gilding; of circular form with a cylindrical neck with slightly everted mouth, and with a deep, oval footrim; cast with a reticulated design on both main sides, with a central medallion framing a coiling scaly dragon flying through scrolling clouds in pursuit of a flaming pearl, surrounded by a wide border of scrolling leaves; the neck with an intertwined scrolling band; a similar band encircling the foot; the narrow sides meeting at a rope-twist edge; with original matching stopper set with coral and jade beads.

Northern China or Mongolia

1800-1900
Height: 6.5 cm

Published: Geng Baochang, *The Appreciation of Chinese Snuff Bottles*, Joint Publishing, Hong Kong, 1992, p. 324.

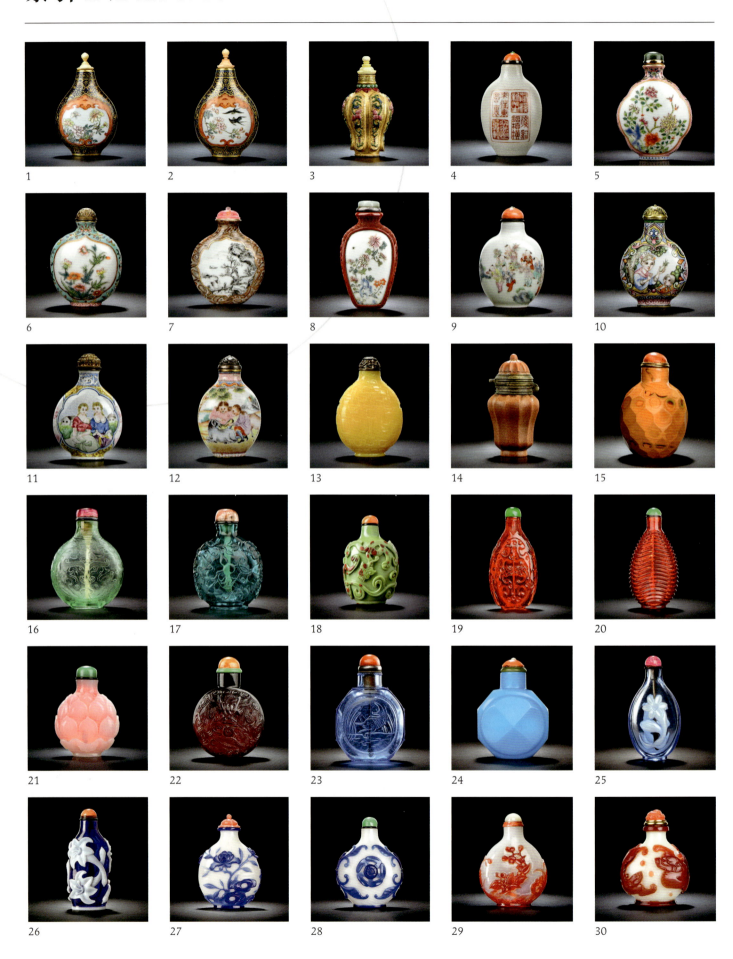

1

2

3

4

5

6

7

8

9

10

11

12

13

14

15

16

17

18

19

20

21

22

23

24

25

26

27

28

29

30

31

32

33

34

35

36

37

38

39

40

41

42

43

44

45

46

47

48

49

50

51

52

53

54

55

56

57

58

59

60

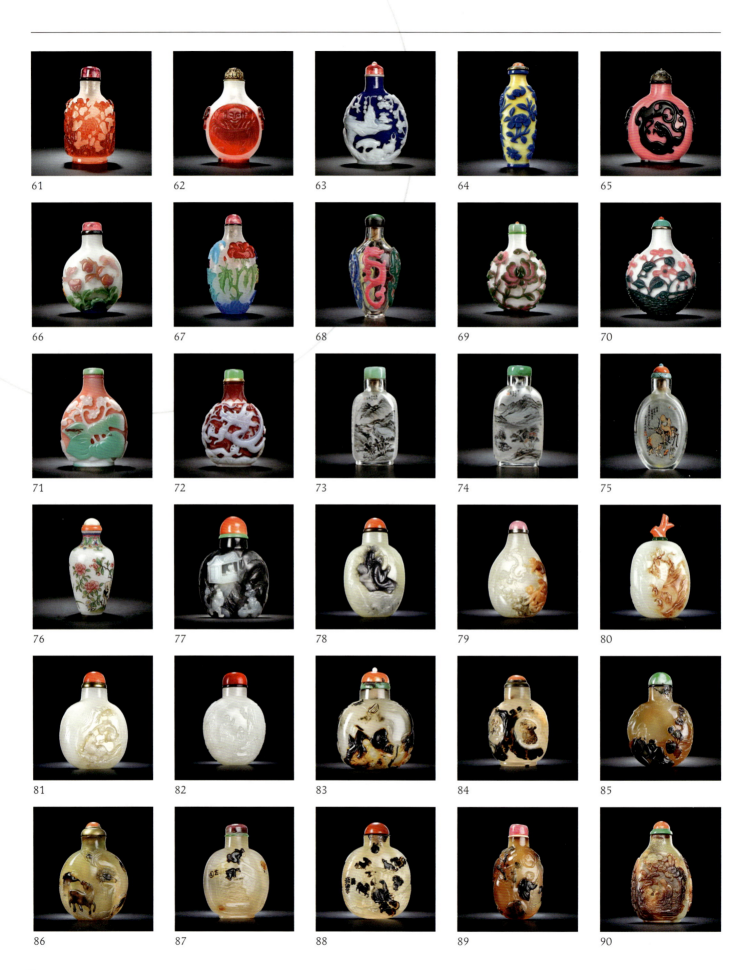

61   62   63   64   65

66   67   68   69   70

71   72   73   74   75

76   77   78   79   80

81   82   83   84   85

86   87   88   89   90

91

92

93

94

95

96

97

98

99

100

101

102

103

104

105

106

107

108

109

110

111

112

113

114

115

116

117

118

119

120

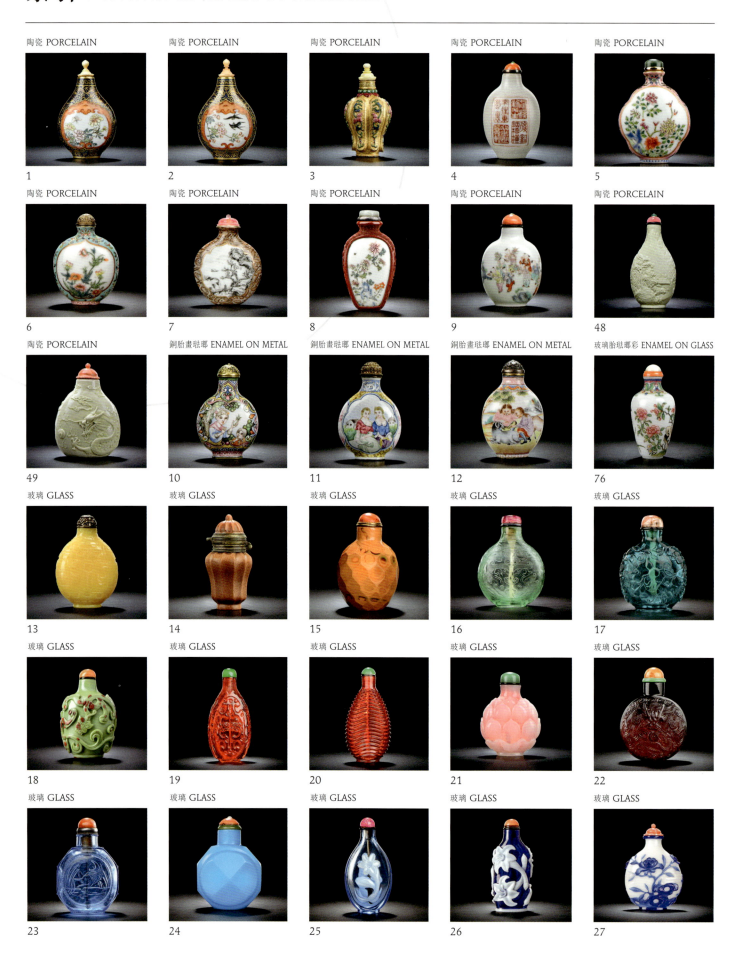

陶瓷 PORCELAIN

1

陶瓷 PORCELAIN

2

陶瓷 PORCELAIN

3

陶瓷 PORCELAIN

4

陶瓷 PORCELAIN

5

陶瓷 PORCELAIN

6

陶瓷 PORCELAIN

7

陶瓷 PORCELAIN

8

陶瓷 PORCELAIN

9

陶瓷 PORCELAIN

48

陶瓷 PORCELAIN

49

銅胎畫琺瑯 ENAMEL ON METAL

10

銅胎畫琺瑯 ENAMEL ON METAL

11

銅胎畫琺瑯 ENAMEL ON METAL

12

玻璃胎琺瑯彩 ENAMEL ON GLASS

76

玻璃 GLASS

13

玻璃 GLASS

14

玻璃 GLASS

15

玻璃 GLASS

16

玻璃 GLASS

17

玻璃 GLASS

18

玻璃 GLASS

19

玻璃 GLASS

20

玻璃 GLASS

21

玻璃 GLASS

22

玻璃 GLASS

23

玻璃 GLASS

24

玻璃 GLASS

25

玻璃 GLASS

26

玻璃 GLASS

27

玻璃 GLASS   玻璃 GLASS   玻璃 GLASS   玻璃 GLASS   玻璃 GLASS

28   29   30   31   50

玻璃 GLASS   玻璃 GLASS   玻璃 GLASS   玻璃 GLASS   玻璃 GLASS

51   52   53   54   55

玻璃 GLASS   玻璃 GLASS   玻璃 GLASS   玻璃 GLASS   玻璃 GLASS

58   59   60   61   62

玻璃 GLASS   玻璃 GLASS   玻璃 GLASS   玻璃 GLASS   玻璃 GLASS

63   64   65   66   67

玻璃 GLASS   玻璃 GLASS   玻璃 GLASS   玻璃 GLASS   玻璃 GLASS

68   69   70   71   72

內畫 INSIDE-PAINTED   內畫 INSIDE-PAINTED   內畫 INSIDE-PAINTED   玉 JADE   玉 JADE

73   74   75   32   33

玉 JADE　玉 JADE　玉 JADE　玉 JADE　玉 JADE

34　35　36　37　38

玉 JADE　玉 JADE　玉 JADE　玉 JADE　玉 JADE

39　40　41　77　78

玉 JADE　玉 JADE　玉 JADE　玉 JADE　玉 JADE

79　80　81　82　90

玉 JADE　玉 JADE　玉 JADE　玉 JADE　玉 JADE

91　92　97　98　99

玉 JADE　玉 JADE　玉 JADE　玉 JADE　玉 JADE

100　101　102　103　104

玉 JADE　玉 JADE　玉 JADE　玉 JADE　玉 JADE

105　106　107　108　109

玉 JADE

110

玉 JADE

111

瑪瑙 AGATE

83

瑪瑙 AGATE

84

瑪瑙 AGATE

85

瑪瑙 AGATE

86

瑪瑙 AGATE

87

瑪瑙 AGATE

88

瑪瑙 AGATE

89

瑪瑙 AGATE

94

瑪瑙 AGATE

95

瑪瑙 AGATE

96

瑪瑙 AGATE

112

瑪瑙 AGATE

133

瑪瑙 AGATE

114

瑪瑙 AGATE

115

瑪瑙 AGATE

116

瑪瑙 AGATE

117

紅白瑪瑙 CARNELIAN

118

瑪瑙 CHALCEDONY

42

瑪瑙 CHALCEDONY

43

瑪瑙 CHALCEDONY

44

羊肝瑪瑙 JASPER

93

碧璽 TOURMALINE

119

有機質料 ORGANIC

45

有機質料 ORGANIC

46

有機質料 ORGANIC

47

有機質料 ORGANIC

56

有機質料 ORGANIC

57

金屬 METAL

120

底款 BASE MARKS

1

2

3

4

5

6

8

9

10

11

12

15

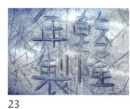

23

24

28

30

39

42

48

49

72

76

參考書目 SELECTED BIBLIOGRAPHY

- *Chinese Snuff Bottles.* Catalogue of an exhibition, 15 October to 26 November 1977. Hong Kong Museum of Art, 1977.《中國鼻烟壺》，香港中國鼻烟壺收藏家學會、香港市政局聯合主辦，香港藝術館，1977年10月15日至11月26日。
- **Chu, Clare.** *Chinese Snuff Bottles from Southern Californian Collectors.* Catalogue of an exhibition at LACMA, Los Angeles, 2016.
- **Chu, Clare.** *50 for 50. Chinese Snuff Bottles from Mid-Atlantic Collectors.* Catalogue of an exhibition at The Walters Art Museum, Baltimore, 2018.
- **Ford, John Gilmore.** *Chinese Snuff Bottles.* The Edward Choate O'Dell Collection. Baltimore: The International Chinese Snuff Bottle Society, 1982.
- **Hall, Robert.** *Chinese Snuff Bottles, Masterpieces from the Rietburg Museum Zurich.* Zurich: Museum Rietburg, 1993.
- **Hall, Robert.** *The Art of the Imperial Addiction, Chinese Snuff Bottles VII.* London: Robert Hall, 1995.
- *Hidden Treasures of the Dragon.* Chinese Snuff Bottles from the Collections of Humphrey K. F. Hui, Margaret Polak, and Christopher C. H. Sin. 龍寶. Catalogue of an exhibition held at the Art Gallery of New South Wales, 19 December 1991 to 27 January 1992. Hong Kong, 1991.
- **Hughes, Michael C.** *The Blair Bequest. Chinese Snuff Bottles from the Princeton University Art Museum.* Hong Kong: The International Chinese Snuff Bottle Society, 2002.
- **Hughes, Michael C.** *The Chester Beatty Library, Dublin. Chinese Snuff Bottles.* Hong Kong: The International Chinese Snuff Bottle Society, 2009.
- *An Imperial Qing Tradition.* An Exhibition of Chinese Snuff Bottles from the Collections of Humphrey K. F. Hui and Christopher C. H. Sin. Catalogue of an exhibition held at the Asian Art Museum of San Francisco, 8 December 1994 to 5 February 1995 and the Phoenix Art Museum, 15 February 1995 to 15 April 1995. Hong Kong, 1994.
- **Hui, Humphrey K. F.** *An Addicted Dedication, Chinese Snuff Bottles, Christopher Sin's Collection.* Hong Kong: CA Design, 2013
- **Jutheau, Viviane.** *Guide du Collectionneur de Tabatieres Chinoises.* Paris: Denoel, 1980.
- **Kleiner, Robert W. L.** *Chinese Snuff Bottles from the Collection of Mary and George Bloch.* Hong Kong: Herald International, 1987.
- **Kleiner, Robert.** *Chinese Snuff Bottles. The White Wings Collection.* Hong Kong: Robert Kleiner, 1997.
- **Kleiner, Robert.** *Treasures from the Sanctum of Enlightened Respect.* Chinese Snuff Bottles from the Collection of Denis Low. Hong Kong: Robert Kleiner, 1999.
- **Kleiner, Robert.** *In Search of a Dragon: Underglaze-Blue and White Porcelain Snuff Bottles from the Collection of Joseph Baruch Silver.* Published to accompany an exhibition at the Gardiner Museum, Toronto, September 5th - November 7th, 2007 and to coincide with the 39th Annual Convention of the International Chinese Snuff Bottle Society. Hong Kong: Robert Kleiner, 2007.
- **Lawrence, Clare.** *The Alexander Brody Collection of Chinese Snuff Bottles.* London: Clare Lawrence, 1995.
- **Lawrence, Clare.** *Chinese Snuff Bottles from the Dick Hardy Collection and Other Sources.* London: Clare Lawrence, 1991.
- **Lawrence, Clare.** *Miniature Masterpieces from the Middle Kingdom. The Monimar Collection of Chinese Snuff Bottles.* London: Zhenliu Xuan Publishing Company, 1996.
- **Lawrence, Clare.** *The Thewlis Collection Chinese Snuff Bottles.* London: Clare Lawrence, 1990.
- **Low, Denis S. K.** *More Treasures from the Sanctum of Enlightened Respect.* Hong Kong: Denis S. K. Low, 2002.
- **Low, Denis S. K.** *Chinese Snuff Bottles from the Sanctum of Enlightened Respect III.* Hong Kong: Asian Civilizations Museum and Lawrence King Publishing Ltd., 2007.

- **Ma Zengshan.** *Inside-Painted Snuff Bottle Artist Ma Shaoxuan [1867-1939]. A Biography and Study.* Hong Kong: The International Chinese Snuff Bottle Society, 1997.
- **Moss, Hugh.** *Snuff Bottles of China.* Illustrating a collection formed by Count Kurt Graf Blucher von Wahlstatt. London: Bibelot, 1971.
- **Moss, Hugh, Victor Graham, and Ka Bo Tsang.** *The Art of the Chinese Snuff Bottle. The J & J Collection.* 2 vols. New York: Weatherhill, 1993.
- **Moss, Hugh, Victor Graham, and Ka Bo Tsang.** *A Treasury of Chinese Snuff Bottles. The Mary and George Bloch Collection. Volume 1, JADE.* Hong Kong: Herald International Ltd., 1995.
- **Moss, Hugh, Victor Graham, and Ka Bo Tsang.** *A Treasury of Chinese Snuff Bottles. The Mary and George Bloch Collection. Volume 2, Part 1 and Part 2, QUARTZ.* Hong Kong: Herald International Ltd., 1998.
- **Moss Hugh, Victor Graham, and Ka Bo Tsang.** *A Treasury of Chinese Snuff Bottles. The Mary and George Bloch Collection. Volume 3, STONES OTHER THAN JADE AND QUARTZ.* Hong Kong: Herald International Ltd., 1998.
- **Moss, Hugh, Victor Graham, and Ka Bo Tsang.** *A Treasury of Chinese Snuff Bottles. The Mary and George Bloch Collection. Volume 4, Part 1 and Part 2, INSIDE PAINTED.* Hong Kong: Herald International Ltd., 2000.
- **Moss, Hugh, Victor Graham, and Ka Bo Tsang.** *A Treasury of Chinese Snuff Bottles. The Mary and George Bloch Collection. Volume 5, Part 1, Part 2 and Part 3, GLASS.* Hong Kong: Herald International Ltd., 2002.
- **Moss, Hugh, Victor Graham, and Ka Bo Tsang.** *A Treasury of Chinese Snuff Bottles. The Mary and George Bloch Collection. Volume 6, Part 1, Part 2, and Part 3, ARTS OF THE FIRE.* Hong Kong: Herald International Ltd., 2008.
- **Moss, Hugh, Victor Graham, and Ka Bo Tsang.** *A Treasury of Chinese Snuff Bottles. The Mary and George Bloch Collection. Volume 7, Part 1 and Part 2, ORGANIC, METAL, MIXED MEDIA.* Hong Kong: Herald International Ltd., 2009.
- **Nicollier, Verene.** *The Baur Collection Geneva Chinese Snuff Bottles.* Geneve, Collections Baur, 2007.
- **Palmer Edwin and Clare Chu.** *The Chepsted Notebook, A Collection of Snuff Bottles.* Seychelles: Edwin Palmer, 2013.
- **Perry, Lilla S.** *Chinese Snuff Bottles. The Adventures and Studies of a Collector.* Rutland, VT, and Tokyo: Charles F. Tuttle, 1960.
- *Snuff Bottles - The Complete Treasures of the Palace Museum* 《故宮博物院藏文物珍品全集》. Volume 47. Hong Kong: The Commercial Press [Hong Kong] Ltd., 2003.
- **Stevens, Bob C.** *The Collector's Book of Snuff Bottles.* New York and Tokyo: Weatherhill, 1976.
- *Tributes from Guangdong to the Qing Court.* Jointly presented by the Palace Museum, Beijing and the Art Gallery, The Chinese University of Hong Kong, 28 February to 12 April 1987. Hong Kong: Art Gallery, Chinese University of Hong Kong, 1987.